The Last Samurai Reread

REREADINGS

REREADINGS

EDITED BY NICHOLAS DAMES AND JENNY DAVIDSON

Short and accessible books by scholars, writers, and critics, each one revisiting a favorite post-1970 novel from the vantage point of the now. Taking a look at novels both celebrated and neglected, the series aims to display the full range of the possibilities of criticism, with books that experiment with form, voice, and method in an attempt to find different paths among scholarship, theory, and creative writing.

The Last Samurai

REREAD

LEE KONSTANTINOU

COLUMBIA UNIVERSITY PRESS

New York

Columbia University Press
Publishers Since 1893
New York   Chichester, West Sussex
cup.columbia.edu
Copyright © 2022 Columbia University Press

Library of Congress Cataloging-in-Publication Data
Names: Konstantinou, Lee, author.
Title: The last samurai reread / Lee Konstantinou.
Description: New York : Columbia University Press, [2022] | Series:
Rereadings | Includes index.
Identifiers: LCCN 2022015194 (print) | LCCN 2022015195 (ebook) |
ISBN 9780231185820 (hardback ; acid-free paper) | ISBN 9780231185837
(trade paperback; acid-free paper) | ISBN 9780231546355 (ebook)
Subjects: LCSH: Dewitt, Helen, 1957– Last samurai. | LCGFT:
Literary criticism.
Classification: LCC PS3554.E92945 L3735 2022 (print) | LCC PS3554.
E92945 (ebook) | DDC 813/.54—dc23/eng/20220502
LC record available at https://lccn.loc.gov/2022015194
LC ebook record available at https://lccn.loc.gov/2022015195

∞

Columbia University Press books are printed on permanent and durable
acid-free paper.
Printed in the United States of America

Cover design: Julia Kushnirsky
Cover illustration: Henry Sene Yee

For Eleanor

Who is the father of any son that any son should love him or he any son?

—James Joyce, *Ulysses*

CONTENTS

Preface

THE LAST SAMURAI, UNREAD

This book should probably be called *The Last Samurai Unread*. After all, Helen DeWitt's debut novel, *The Last Samurai*, which was published more than twenty years ago, has yet to be read for the first time by many readers, including many literary critics. When I mentioned I was writing about the novel, I found myself forced to explain, on more than one occasion, that the book has nothing to do with the 2003 Tom Cruise film of the same name. No actual samurai appear in DeWitt's novel. Mostly set in London in the 1980s and 1990s but global in the geographic and linguistic range of its imagination, the novel follows the story of a brilliant and eccentric former classics scholar, Sibylla Newman, an American, who lives in poverty and tries to raise her son, Ludo, by herself. She refuses to introduce the boy to his father, a vapid and thoughtless travel writer with whom she had a one-night stand, and she refuses to return to her family in the United States. The boy is brilliant. He reads Homer in the original at age nine and learns advanced mathematics by reading Schaum's Outline Series on Laplace transforms and Fourier analysis. Only one Japanese character appears in the book, an avant-garde pianist. The main samurai mentioned are characters in Akira Kurosawa's classic 1954 film *Seven Samurai*.

Sibylla regards the film as a masterpiece and watches it again and again on a VHS tape. One day, she reads a newspaper article that suggests that "in the absence of a benevolent male, the single mother faces an uphill battle in raising her son. It is essential that she provide the boy with male role models—neighbours, or uncles, or friends of the family, to share their interests and hobbies."[1] And she decides, "Well, if L needs a role model let him watch Seven Samurai & he will have 8." Eight role models: the film's six samurai, one man who poses as a samurai, and one brave farmer who recruits them. The choice of *Seven Samurai* seems at first arbitrary and half serious, an attempt by Sibylla to rationalize not introducing Ludo to his father. Yet with each viewing, each attempt to explain the choice of Kurosawa, the conceit takes on greater weight. The film becomes a rich metaphorical resource for Sibylla and for Ludo— and for the novel.

Sibylla introduces her son to the film and, at his insistence, teaches him Japanese. When Ludo does meet his biological father, he's terribly disappointed in the man. "I can't say I'm his son, because it's true," he concludes (280). Inspired by the example of *Seven Samurai*, he sets out on a quest to find a replacement father, testing each candidate in the same way that the aging ronin Kambei tests candidate samurai in Kurosawa's film. A line from the film, "A good samurai will parry the blow," becomes a mantra for Ludo and provides titles for six chapters in the fifth part of the novel. Ludo believes that a true father, like a true samurai, will parry his figurative blows. Unfortunately, each candidate Ludo encounters fails—he becomes a type, a routine, a cliché of masculinity—and so Ludo's quest begins anew, looping back to the start.

The boy's quest is, in a sense, quixotic, doomed to fail in advance, yet in his determined refusal to settle for a bad father we can see the core dialectic of *The Last Samurai*. One must, the book suggests, face reality honestly but never submit to that reality. We must judge what exists, what is given, what we unthinkingly take as natural or necessary or conventional by the most stringent standards of analysis—not by the standard of what exists but by the standard of what might become possible in a better, more rational world. When we marry our wildest desires to the highest standards, we thereby test our reality.

A good reality will parry the blow.

❖   ❖   ❖

The Last Samurai was well received when it was published in 2000, but it has not found a widespread readership. After its publisher, Talk

Miramax Books, was dissolved in 2005, the book went out of print. Few scholars have written about it. Nonetheless, the novel has gathered a small but influential coterie of advocates. Those who've read *The Last Samurai* have tended to love it, to obsess over it, to shove it into the hands of friends and acquaintances. After a brief time out of print, the book was republished by New Directions in 2016 and has subsequently been hailed by *New York* magazine as the best book of the twenty-first century.

I first read the book in 2007, thinking I might want to include it in a project I was writing about novelists who were trying to move beyond postmodernism. DeWitt was associated with authors such as David Foster Wallace and Jonathan Franzen, and she has suggested that her book belongs alongside these generational peers.[2] I initially wanted to write a chapter pairing *The Last Samurai* with Jonathan Safran Foer's *Extremely Loud and Incredibly Close* (2005) and to discuss the role that the figure of the "knowing child" plays in twenty-first-century fiction.

But as Rich Beck notes, DeWitt's novel may seem to belong to the "Precocious Child" genre, but it also ruthlessly "obviates it," as if *The Last Samurai* were "written, point by point, to reject everything the Precocious Child novel would come to stand for."[3] Reading the novel in the closing days of 2007, I found the book's Precocious Child less gripping than its Precarious Mother. *The Last Samurai* found a way to speak to the feeling of living at a time when economic crisis was laying waste to many lives. *The Last Samurai* was, of course, not about the 2007–2008 financial crisis. But it is about the kind of world where a crisis like that *could* happen, where it *had* happened in different forms, and where it was likely to happen again, unfolding along predictably irrational lines.

Academics certainly didn't have it any worse than others who face the perils of the labor market. But as DeWitt's novel shows, there's a specific experience of the market scholars face. When many of my friends and I started grad school, many assumed or were assured that finding a good—or any—academic job wouldn't pose too much of a problem. Yet even before the financial crisis, there was a dawning sense that these assumptions were mistaken, that many of us would fail to find employment in the profession we had been training to join, that the profession to which we had become attached was not what we thought it was.

And then came the crisis, and the medieval institution of the university encountered the woodchipper of austerity budgets and financialization, which shredded the thoughtless security of many who hoped to pursue an intellectual vocation. The crisis destroyed brilliant academic careers before they could begin, shunting the smartest scholars of a generation into writing occasional essays, often for no pay, on web-based "little magazines," publishing groundbreaking monographs while unemployed or underemployed. Many would agree with Lauren Berlant that they lived within a situation of "cruel optimism," a situation that plants booby traps within one's very conception of the good life.[4] "Cruel optimism" seemed an apt name for the paradoxical attachments many of us held fast to, even as the world seemed to crumble around us. It's a good name, too, for the double binds that burden the characters in *The Last Samurai*.

I made my way through the crisis and managed to find employment in the academy. I didn't write about DeWitt for my first academic book, but I kept track of the author, reading everything I could get my hands on. I wrote a review of *Lightning Rods* for the *Los Angeles Review of Books* and interviewed DeWitt for that publication. I reviewed her short-story collection *Some Trick* for *Public Books*. When I pitched this book, I did so because I wanted to convince more readers and critics to read and write about *The Last Samurai*. I want to lay part of the groundwork for the future study of the novel, to describe its central themes and think about some of the important questions the book raises. Doing so, I hope, will not only teach us something new about DeWitt's book but also help us better understand fiction in an era of escalating income inequality, corporate conglomeration, and precarity.[5] I wanted to offer an original interpretation of *The Last Samurai* but also to understand how the book came into the world, to write a biography of the book. The story of the book, I suspected, might also indirectly be the story of our time.

My approach is inspired by the example of literary critics and sociologists such as Amy Hungerford, Clayton Childress, Matthew Kirschenbaum, William Deresiewicz, Paulo Lemos Horta, and Álvaro Santana-Acuña.[6] These scholars assume, as Hungerford puts it, that our literary life is embodied in "efforts to make literature and make a living, efforts that in the cutthroat world of international capitalism must come and go as quickly as streaming headlines."[7] They show why critics should attend to the ground-level reality of literary institutions, including publishers, agents, etc., as well as to how artists find a way to survive another day and make more art. As Merve Emre has suggested, scholars of contemporary literature who share this assumption might use a range of methods not normally associated with literary criticism—such as oral history, questionnaires, and ethnography—to interrogate the relationship between the contingent factors that bring literature into the world and the literature itself. That is, literary scholars might look to sociology not for its conclusions but for its methods.[8]

I spoke to many people who contributed to the story of *The Last Samurai*. I conducted interviews with DeWitt; DeWitt's former husband, David Levene; her editor at Talk Miramax Books, Jonathan Burnham; the production manager who worked with DeWitt at Talk Miramax, Kristin Powers; and her friends Tim Schmidt and Maude Chilton. The pages that follow develop an interpretation of *The Last Samurai* while giving a chronicle of its composition and publication history. I argue that these two seemingly disparate perspectives—one intrinsic, the other extrinsic—are connected in a significant way for the novel. To be sure, many novelists struggle to finish books and find publishers, but fewer turn that struggle into the subject of their art. *The Last Samurai* does, connecting its struggle to find an audience to the larger question of how one might pursue a nonalienated intellectual life under economic and social conditions of perpetual economic crisis. Ludo's quixotic quest for a better father metaphorically replicates DeWitt's quest, also perhaps quixotic, for a good publisher. Both quests produce situations of cruel optimism. Both test the limits of existing habits, norms, standards, and practices in pursuit of a better life.

In *The Last Samurai*, DeWitt engages in an allegorical and metafictional sort of life writing, though not in the manner of autofiction, a genre that has lately become popular. The "life" she chronicles isn't her own life but the life of her book. In a sense, DeWitt asks us to personify her novel. She invites us to see Sibylla's effort to raise Ludo as an allegory for DeWitt's own efforts to write her novel. But the allegory is uneasy, almost contradictory. Raising Ludo is, after all, what *prevents* Sibylla from completing her intellectual labors and finding fulfillment. Yet Ludo's successful completion of his quest is also what marks DeWitt's own success as a novelist. The boy is both an obstacle to Sibylla's flourishing and its final realization.

In personifying her book in this way, DeWitt opens many avenues for reading the novel. DeWitt arguably has a feminist point to make. She foregrounds the devaluation of unpaid reproductive labor—the labor of child rearing and pedagogy—analogizing these activities to the stultifying work Sibylla must do to make ends meet. The stunted men in Sibylla's life and broken educational institutions that support their careless dominance foist the burden of raising Ludo onto her. Broken institutions also fill her days with endless busywork, interrupting thought, "kill[ing] the mind" that might write a book like *The Last Samurai*.[9] At the same time, DeWitt challenges the historic association of intellectual labor and genres such as encyclopedic fiction with masculinity. That is, while Sibylla might discover she has the responsibility for raising Ludo, this doesn't mean she's particularly well suited to the task or that raising a child represents anything other than a dissipation of her potential. I'll offer a more detailed account of how DeWitt personifies her novel in the chapters ahead, but what I want to underscore is that *The Last Samurai*'s metafictional commentary is also a form of social, political, and institutional critique.

The Last Samurai dreams of a world in which nonalienated intellectual production is possible for all people. It also hopes for the possibility of a nonalienated reception. That is, *The Last Samurai* seeks to discover (or make) an ideal reader who would be improved through her encounter with the novel, despite social pressures and institutions that cordon off the novel from other zones of life. In a world where the imagined purpose of the novel is to entertain or furnish meanings—not to teach or spark further inquiry—*The Last Samurai* dissents, imagining itself to have a pedagogical function. It tries to illustrate what it would mean for a novel to have the power to inspire readers to, for example, realize they can easily learn Greek or Japanese. It asks readers to see in Ludo's brilliance a figure for their own intellectual and aesthetic potential.

The following chapters move (more or less) chronologically through the story of the book's composition, publication, and reception, tying moments of this story to moments in the novel. My first chapter discusses the origin of the novel as a wish-fulfillment fantasy—the fantasy that one could choose one's own father—and the way the novel navigates this fantasy. Chapter 2 considers DeWitt's intellectual history. It discusses her academic dissertation on propriety as a standard of evaluation in ancient Greek and Roman literary criticism, relating her analysis of this ancient standard to her vision of the future of the novel. The third chapter discusses DeWitt's experience with her publisher, Talk Miramax Books, which was founded by Harvey and Bob Weinstein. This chapter elaborates the claim that *The Last Samurai* represents the double bind of authors in an age of corporate conglomeration. Chapter 4 investigates the much-discussed fight DeWitt had with her copyeditor. It uses this fight as an occasion to understand why the novel's nonstandard usage and typography was so important to DeWitt's vision for the book and her investment in statistics, probability, and information design. The final chapter discusses the aftermath of the novel's publication for DeWitt and asks what her ultimate relation to her time is. What does DeWitt's experience teach us about the status of the novel at the end of the twentieth century and the beginning of the twenty-first? What kinds of novels can be published within established literary institutions, and what does the story of *The Last Samurai* reveal about alternative ways of thinking about untapped possibilities of literary art? I conclude with a brief discussion of DeWitt's second novel, *Lightning Rods*, and reflect on what this book's representation of capitalism might tell us about *The Last Samurai*. All told, each chapter highlights how DeWitt's great novel opens out onto economic, social, and political questions of ultimate importance.

The Last Samurai
Reread

1

A LITTLE POTBOILER

I

Helen DeWitt started writing *The Last Samurai* in September 1995. Six years out of a classics doctoral program at Oxford University, she was living in London and working for a temp agency as a legal secretary. In her spare time, she was trying to write a long and structurally complex novel called "The Magnificent Stranger." DeWitt had already written three hundred single-spaced pages of that manuscript, but it was impossible to work on the project while also holding down a job. She needed uninterrupted blocks of time to figure out how to finish the book, and so she decided to take a chance.

She quit and planned to live off her savings. She would write full time.

But after quitting, it proved difficult to make progress. Her hard drive was already a graveyard of unfinished and abandoned projects. Weeks passed, and she found she wasn't getting much writing done. Instead, she sat on the floor for long stretches of time, alone in her flat. One day, during this period of paralysis and growing despair, she talked to her father in the United States. Over the long-distance line, he began hectoring her for not being sufficiently hopeful about her life—which, DeWitt told me, did little to kindle hope in her.

Her father had a unique talent, she recalled, of reminding you that—however depressed you might think you were—deeper basements of hopelessness were available to you. Nearing a new bottom, DeWitt reflected on the fact that you can't pick your parents. Certainly, if *she* had ever been given the chance, she would have chosen someone different. Sitting on the floor of the flat, back against the wall, brooding on her miserable relationship with her father and the creative impasse she had reached, something was dislodged within her.

What would it mean, she wondered, for a child to select his father? It was "a completely preposterous idea," but one that captured her, blooming in her mind, filling her with enthusiasm.[1] What sort of adult would be a plausible candidate for surrogate fatherhood? What education might allow the child to make an informed decision? And at what age would this lucky child, on the one hand, be capable of making a serious choice while, on the other, be young enough to have that choice be meaningful? After all, the point of choosing one's father should be, at the very least, to be *raised* by that father, to discover who you were, who you might become, through the medium of good parenting.

Now *this* was an idea she could work with. Here's what she would do: She would write a book about a child who puts different candidate fathers to the test. The boy would tell each man he was their son. Each would embody a different conception of excellence or masculine virtue, and the narrative would run through each model before settling on a final father who could meet the boy's exacting standards. Different candidates would respond differently to the boy's deception. Some would not recognize his duplicity. Others would see through the ploy and reject the child. Still others would recognize the boy's game but offer guidance. These possibilities would develop logically from the premise of the novel.

From the beginning, the boy's story was entangled with Akira Kurosawa's *Seven Samurai* (1954). The ambiguous figure of a good samurai would serve as an analogy for a good father, and Kurosawa's masterpiece would offer imaginative resources for the novel DeWitt now very much wanted to write.

The novel was initially called "The Seventh Samurai." It would, DeWitt told me, be "a little potboiler."[2] She was sure she could finish a draft in a month. Six weeks at most! Sure, she had previously failed to finish novels. But this time would be different. This time, she would finish the book, try to sell her little novel, and if she was successful, use the proceeds to buy time to complete "The Magnificent Stranger."

This, anyway, was the plan.

II

Writing the novel would take a little longer than six weeks, and the final book would expand to over five hundred pages, confronting DeWitt with just as many structural problems as the novel she had abandoned. Several factors stymied her hopes of quickly writing her "little potboiler." DeWitt offers her own accounts of these challenges, but the novel's origin as a wish-fulfillment fantasy was destined to come into conflict with DeWitt's desire to rigorously elaborate that fantasy, to render the fantasy plausible.

The character of the boy's mother posed a special challenge in this regard. DeWitt's original vision for the book, as a novel about a boy's quest for a surrogate father, ultimately remained in the final version. But the story of his mother became much more important. In the published novel, the mother, Sibylla, is the brilliant daughter of a musically talented mother and intellectually gifted father. Despite their great potential, her parents end up squandering their gifts and running a motel chain in the United States. Sibylla's life in the United States is miserable. Hoping to escape "Motelland and live among rational beings," she lies her way into Oxford and briefly studies classics there before discovering fewer rational beings than she expected among her fellow scholars (23). She quits Oxford and starts working for an academic press in London.

When an American conglomerate buys that small press, Sibylla is invited to a party where she meets a vapid, casually thoughtless travel writer. Despite her scorn for the man, she sleeps with him and becomes pregnant. Determined not to let her son squander his life, Sibylla homeschools him. She teaches him Attic Greek, Japanese, Old Norse, Arabic, aerodynamics, mathematics, and other subjects. The boy's a quick study, a prodigy, possibly a genius.

In DeWitt's original conception of the novel, the mother was named Ruth and was "a Shavian character of perfect self-possession" who remained "sublimely untroubled" in the face of a world at odds with her strong opinions.[3] She was a feminist iconoclast who was firmly convinced that homeschooling her son—and modeling his education on the education of J. S. Mill—was self-evidently a good idea. She fervidly defended her exacting if idiosyncratic standards against all contrary views. Ruth wrote in clear, punchy, well-reasoned prose:

> Well, then, I will write as if for an intelligent six-year-old, who likes the fact that there are facts and wants everything explained. I will explain everything. I will explain Mozart and Bernini and Cezanne and Einstein; I will even explain Jeeves. That is for the comfort of future centuries. I will argue everything: that is for the profit of my own century. And for my own comfort I will think of what can be done with a preface. Glenn Gould (eccentric, brilliant mid-20th century Canadian pianist and specialist in the works of Bach [17th century German composer of genius]) recorded The Well-Tempered Clavier [WTC], and he remarked that the preludes had no real musical interest, they were 'merely prefatory'. And yet even these merely prefatory pieces are recorded so that every note seems premeditated. I will try to do no worse by my merely prefatory material.[4]

This paragraph comes from the preface of an early draft of the novel. It recounts many of the same events as the published book and includes many identical sentences. It's linear, coherent, forceful, and—as DeWitt came to realize—lifeless on the page.

The published version of this passage takes a slightly different form:

> And who was Rilke and who was Zweig and who was Musil? Who was Newton and who was Einstein? Rilke

> Why don't you teach me the syllabaries?
> WHY DON'T YOU TEACH ME THE SYLLABARIES?
> WHY DON'T YOU TEACH ME THE SYLLABARIES?
> Well
> Are they hard?
> Not very
> Please
> Well

Please
I told you the deal
Heiskaienenekontasyllabic duokaienenekontasyllabic

Glenn Gould (eccentric, brilliant mid-20th-century Canadian pianist and specialist in the works of J. S. Bach [18th-century German

HEPTAKAIENENEKONTASYLLABIC

composer of genius]) said of The Well-Tempered Clavier [forget it], that
the preludes

OKTOKAIENENEKONTASYLLABIC

(37)

Rigorously well balanced, stately paragraphs shred into spindly fragments. The mother is trying to explain something but is constantly being interrupted. The boy recombines Greek numerical prefixes to create new adjectives. The son's incessant questions—*Who was X? Who was Y? Why don't you Z?*—create a tempo of agitation and interruption not only for the mother but also for the reader. Greek-derived numerical prefixes bludgeon the listener. The mind of this new version of Ludo's mother can barely sustain a thought, let alone explain everything. In the contrast between these two versions of the same passage, we see the difference between writing "as if for an intelligent six-year-old" and writing while doing the unpaid reproductive labor of taking care of an intelligent six-year-old, the difference between writing without interruption and writing while having to do other work.

DeWitt renamed the mother "Sibylla," after the epigraph of *The Waste Land*: "'Nam Sibyllam quidem Cumis ego ipse oculis meis vidi in ampulla pendere, et cum illi pueri dicerent: Σίβυλλα τί θέλεις; respondebat illa: ἀποθανεῖν θέλω.'"[5] Citing Petronius's *Satyricon*, Eliot refers to a story about the priestess presiding over the Apollonian oracle at Cumae. As legend tells, Apollo offered to grant a wish to the Cumaean Sibyl in exchange for her virginity. The Sibyl wished for unnaturally long life, as many years as there are grains in a handful of sand, but the god did not grant her eternal youth, so her body withered away until she fit in a jar or cage, leaving behind only her voice. In *The Satyricon*, the former slave Trimalchio recounts the story of his encounter with the Sibyl. "I myself with my own eyes saw the Sibyl hanging in a cage; and when the boys cried at her: 'Sibyl, Sibyl, what do you want?' [she would answer] 'I would that I were dead.'"[6]

Ruth is a model of assurance.

Sibylla, a character named after a victim of divine abuse, *wants to die*.

In the new version of the novel that was emerging, Ludo's part of the story retained the tidy structure of a fable, each new father considered and discarded as if the boy (and DeWitt) were working through the arguments of a logical proof. But the mother's story was increasingly a hot mess, told in fragmented and digressive chapters, interpolated flashbacks, comic dialogues, interrupted commentaries on art, philosophy, classical scholarship, film. As Sibylla became more central to the novel—as central as Ludo, if not more—the novel became correspondingly harder to write.

III

The other challenge was financial. In October 1995, DeWitt ran out of money, and "The Seventh Samurai" was hardly begun. Instead of going back to a temp agency, she made an independent arrangement with the London office of an American law firm, Cravath, Swaine & Moore, to work as a legal secretary and paralegal. She worked the night shift and wrote during the day. At the firm, she met an American lawyer, Tim Schmidt, who had just moved to London from New York with his wife.

Schmidt recalls that he first noticed DeWitt because she was reading an Arabic newspaper with three different colored highlighters in hand— she was trying to learn the language, she told him.[7] Schmidt asked around the office and learned from colleagues that the legal secretary was writing a novel. No one had asked her what the book was about. "Everybody was a little bit intimidated by her," Schmidt told me. He asked

DeWitt about the book, and she was eager to talk about it. He told her that he would love to read it when it was ready. The next day, she gave him two chapters, drawn from Ludo's part of the novel.

Though he'd asked to see the manuscript, Schmidt was afraid to read it. What if he hated it? After sitting on the chapters for a week, he worked up the courage to read them and was hugely impressed. He asked his wife, Maude Chilton, for a second opinion, telling her nothing about his own views, and she also loved the sample. Schmidt and Chilton wanted to help DeWitt find a publisher, so they connected her to a friend, the newly minted literary agent Stephanie Cabot.

Cabot was working at the William Morris Agency in London, and she took on DeWitt as a client. She sent out a partial draft of the novel to editors, hoping to win an advanced contract. The responses were mixed. Editors would like one part of the manuscript but not another. Some thought the sample was intimidating and emotionally cold. Many expressed enthusiasm—but enthusiasm didn't turn into an advance. What DeWitt wanted was enough money to work full time on the book, but now she was dividing her days between writing the book and working up proposals to earn an advance. She was constantly being interrupted, and the interruptions worked their way into the novel, in the form of Ludo's interruptions of his mother.

One offer of £7,500 materialized, from Rebecca Wilson, an editor at the UK-based publisher Weidenfeld & Nicholson. But the offer did not satisfy DeWitt. "I tried to imagine getting Greek typeset," she explained, "getting Japanese typeset, with this editor and thought: if I go through with this I will commit suicide within six months."[8] After eighteen months of shopping the novel, DeWitt recalls, she was growing increasingly "insane."[9]

DeWitt parted ways with Cabot, and after talking with a series of other agents decided—in 1998—to shelve "The Seventh Samurai" even though the manuscript was completed. She would move on to new novels, short novels, structurally simple ones. She would live cheaply, write one novel a month for a year, try to sell them, and try again to sell "The Seventh Samurai" on more favorable terms after she had published other, simpler books. She moved from London to Chesterfield in the East

Midlands and lived in a terraced house for £60 a week. There, she completed her satirical second novel, *Lightning Rods*, and worked on other books. But it was the novel she had thought she set aside that found a publisher first.

DeWitt's friendship with Schmidt and Chilton proved decisive. Chilton, who was a filmmaker, optioned the rights for *Lightning Rods*. She happened to be the sister of Harvey Weinstein's first wife, Eve Chilton. In the late 1990s, riding a wave of critical and commercial success, having won a Best Picture Oscar for their adaptation of *The English Patient*, the Weinstein brothers were expanding their media empire. They were drifting away from the quality indies that had made their reputation into "mid-range, star-driven 'Oscar bait'" more akin to *The English Patient*, and—synergy in their eyes—they had ambitious plans to get into magazines, book publishing, and television.[10] Talk Miramax Books was a spinoff of Tina Brown's *Talk* magazine, bankrolled by Miramax and the Hearst Corporation. The inaugural editor of Talk Miramax, Jonathan Burnham, read the manuscript of *Lightning Rods* but passed on it. Then he read "The Seventh Samurai" and fell in love.

Burnham initially offered a $70,000 advance. DeWitt negotiated the contract with Talk Miramax without an agent, though she had a lawyer look over the terms of the deal. Burnham brought the manuscript to the Frankfurt Book Fair in 1999, selling the translation rights to twenty countries—a wild success. In the United Kingdom, Chatto & Windus bought the novel, beating Faber & Faber and Picador at auction. DeWitt was able to secure final approval over the published manuscript but was also given responsibility for securing permissions. Securing those rights proved to be extremely nettlesome—the Kurosawa estate allowed her to use quotations from *Seven Samurai* but refused to let her use the title "The Seventh Samurai." The copyediting process would also become a nightmarish slog for everyone involved.

Despite these challenges, late in the year 2000, the book was published with its new title, *The Last Samurai*. The novel was praised when it appeared, earning admiring reviews in the *New Yorker*, the *New York Times*, *New York* magazine, and the *New York Review of Books*. Yet there was a note of hesitation even in reviews that praised the novel. In her

New Yorker review, A. S. Byatt admires DeWitt for offering a "genuinely new story, a genuinely new form, which has more to offer on every reading but is gripping from the beginning of the first."[11] There's a hint of special pleading in the promise that the book is immediately "gripping," as though she were afraid some readers might be bored by the book on a first reading but didn't want to say so openly. Writing in the *New York Review of Books*, Daniel Mendelson strongly admired Sibylla's sections of the novel but suggested that "the Ludo material comes off as ventriloquized and approximate."[12] Despite this relatively strong showing, the book seemed fated—as the cover copy of the hardback edition predicted—to become (little more than) a "cult classic," another erudite literary novel more often cited than read. Burnham was disappointed with the book's initial reception.[13] It won no literary prizes, though it was shortlisted for the Orange Prize. Even so, one judge on the committee said that "*The Last Samurai* . . . seems at first sight flashy and a little overly clever, but the more we read it the more we admired the world [DeWitt] had created."[14] Not exactly unalloyed praise. The process of publishing *The Last Samurai*, by DeWitt's account, left her crushed: A decade of "breakdowns, clinical depression, brushes with suicide" would follow the arrival of the novel into the world.[15]

IV

Though a hundred thousand copies of the first edition of *The Last Samurai* were sold, DeWitt struggled to publish subsequent books. She was contracted to write a design-intensive nonfiction book on poker for Talk Miramax but was unable to complete the manuscript. In 2008, she self-published *Your Name Here*, coauthored with the journalist Ilya Gridneff, on her website. A decade after she finished it, she published *Lightning Rods* with New Directions in 2011. After Talk Miramax was absorbed into Disney's Hyperion and shuttered, the rights to *The Last Samurai* became available again, and New Directions republished the book in 2016. Across her career, DeWitt has confronted a series of difficult relationships with agents, editors, and publishers, some of which are dramatized in the stories of her collection *Some Trick: Thirteen Stories*, published by New Directions in 2018. The critic sympathetic to DeWitt's artistic achievement might be tempted to place all the blame for these difficult relationships on the agents, editors, and publishers whom DeWitt has worked with. But even DeWitt's own representation of the struggle of her characters makes clear that these difficult relationships go both ways: the institutions DeWitt has worked with have, in many ways, failed to give her what she has needed as an artist. But DeWitt has also made demands of these institutions that they have not been equipped to meet. DeWitt has, by her own admission, expected these institutions to conform to a fantasy of how she thinks they *should* work, not how they actually work. One might spend many pages apportioning blame in particular cases of institutional failure. We might wonder whether the institutions in question should have been able to accommodate her demands or whether her requests were unreasonable. But such judgment notwithstanding, DeWitt's writing can fruitfully be read as a sustained meditation on her perennial disappointment, justified or not, with the publishing industry. Many stories feature bad middlemen—vapid agents, manipulative gallery owners, and ignorant critics. These stories invite us to read the struggles of characters who wrestle with irrational artistic institutions as allegories of larger contemporary social, political, and economic dysfunctions. At the broadest level, even if we think our existing artistic institutions work just fine, DeWitt's stories dramatize how and why institutions can fail artists. And they struggle to imagine what shape a different artistic world might take.

There are signs that a wider readership might finally be recognizing DeWitt. The novelist has long enjoyed support among a handful of prominent critics. *Your Name Here* was, quite unusually for a self-published novel, reviewed in the *London Review of Books*, and an excerpt of it appeared in *n+1*. *Lightning Rods* received many positive reviews, and the rerelease of *The Last Samurai* was favorably received. In a review of *Some Trick*, James Wood wrote about *The Last Samurai* as if it were already established as a great novel (though he had never written about it before).[16] And in September 2018, a panel of critics convened by *New York* magazine chose *The Last Samurai* as "Best Book of the Century (for Now)."

Christian Lorentzen, long a champion of DeWitt's work, wrote the note for *The Last Samurai*. He had previously written an admiring profile of the author in *New York* magazine, declaring *The Last Samurai* and *Lightning Rods* to be "two of the finest novels published this century."[17]

In his write-up for *New York*, Lorentzen notes that it has taken some time for DeWitt's achievement to be recognized. He isn't sure how to explain this neglect. On the one hand, he proposes that "it's an accident of recent history that it's taken the culture some time to realize" that *The Last Samurai* is a masterpiece.[18] At the same time, he admits that the novel "was never easily subsumed in one of the day's critical categories." When he argues for the importance of the book, Lorentzen says the novel is both "singular" and "a story of our time." What makes it a story of our time is its focus on the economic struggles of its main characters. Sibylla and Ludo fight to make ends meet—and a life worth living—in their unheated London flat. What makes the novel singular is its idiosyncratic dedication to showcasing the world's knowledge. The interplay between the book's timeliness and its lack of fit with its time—and the concomitant interplay between the lowness of its characters' material circumstances and the splendor of its intellectual commitments—are for Lorentzen what make it an arresting, important book. It's a book that "strives to take in the whole world from the vantage point of material deprivation," an autodidactic, encyclopedic narrative from below.

DeWitt has clearly come a long way from the floor of her London flat, yet literary scholars have written very little about *The Last Samurai*.[19] More has been written on *Lightning Rods*, whose satire of neoliberalism and corporate feminism is more easily assimilated with current critical priorities. When it has been discussed, *The Last Samurai* has largely been written about as if it were part of the postmodern tradition. It's often taken as an example of one of the most prestigious postmodern genres, encyclopedic narrative, "an almost super-canonical form, yet one that is virtually unread."[20] Sam Anderson has called *The Last Samurai* a "meganovel."[21] *The Last Samurai* was the subject of a group read at Veronica Esposito's literary blog *Conversational Reading* (in the manner of Infinite Summer, dedicated to David Foster Wallace, or #OccupyGaddis). Contemporary encyclopedic narrative is typically defined by its length, its eager incorporation of technological and scientific rhetoric, its formal difficulty, and its ambition to make an all-encompassing artistic statement about the character of contemporary life.[22] And it is overwhelmingly assumed to be a masculine genre.

Critics who celebrate the encyclopedic novel have argued that DeWitt not only belongs to this tradition but has broadened its gender profile. Steven Moore begins his *Washington Post* review, for example, by explaining that "the learned novel is mostly a guy thing."[23] DeWitt has, he suggests, "crashed this boys club," and "*The Last Samurai* will crown DeWitt this year's It Girl of postmodernism." Sven Birkerts highlights DeWitt as a writer who is "writing determinedly outside the domestic pigeonhole (old stereotypes live on)" and can "match their male colleagues in inventiveness and a willingness to take on the zeitgeist."[24] Stephen Burn has suggested that *The Last Samurai* is an emblem of the "broadening" of the encyclopedic tradition to include authors other than straight white men.[25] The all-male panel of judges who shortlisted the book for the Orange Prize describe the book in similar terms. The book is, according to one summary of the deliberations for the prize, a "bravura grandstand of intellectualism, which eschews plot and character to revel in the sheer delight of languages and obscure learning." *The Last Samurai* is "a witty, smart, cerebral book" that "appeals to the brains and a sense of the absurd rather than to the heart and reader/character empathy."[26] "Pack[ing] an emotional punch," we learn, is "not DeWitt's game." DeWitt is also passive-aggressively praised for being, perhaps, too much like male novelists who are guilty of "show[ing] off in their writing, putting their logo on the text, never allowing the reader to forget them."[27]

These are not incorrect assessments—DeWitt *does* have encyclopedic ambitions—but there are problems with this line of interpretation. First, these critics generally ignore or minimize important encyclopedic works by women such as Gertrude Stein's *The Making of Americans* (1925), Doris Lessing's *The Golden Notebook* (1962), Margaret Young's *Miss Macintosh, My Darling* (1965), Leslie Marmon Silko's *Almanac of the Dead* (1991), Gayl Jones's *Mosquito* (1999), and Karen Tei Yamashita's *I Hotel* (2010).

They note the historic association of intellect with masculinity and emotion with femininity but simply reverse the terms for DeWitt, suggesting that, after all, women too can be intellectuals! What they don't do is challenge the idea that there's a hard barrier between intellect and emotion. A cerebral novel is not, apparently, one that can make us feel much of anything, especially when it risks doing little more than showing off the chilly cognitive horsepower of its author. But this is a distinction that *The Last Samurai* challenges. Our intellectual life, no less than other parts of human life, is profoundly wrapped up with emotion. Our attachment to a mathematical puzzle can consume us. Our commitment to argumentative rigor has the power to save us—or, in some cases, destroy us. The question of whether we fulfill our intellectual potential can be a matter of life and death.

In demonstrating the inseparability of intellect and emotion, DeWitt challenges a common contemporary assumption about the nature and function of literary fiction, the assumption that it's better if novelists wear their intellectual commitments and learning lightly. The critic Marco Roth is therefore right to say that DeWitt is "the 21st century's best 18th century novelist."[28] Roth's comment suggests, on the one hand, that DeWitt invokes the satirical spirit of the eighteenth century—indeed, DeWitt has affirmed her love of Swift, Pope, Voltaire, and Diderot. On the other hand, the quip suggests that DeWitt embraces the didactic commitment of these writers to delight and instruct.[29] Roth's comment also highlights how DeWitt writes as if the congealed literary categories of our moment do not apply to her. We live at the culmination of a long literary history of specialization, where novelists are minted in the university in much the same way as research scientists and engineers and where didacticism is thought to be antithetical to good art. DeWitt seems to disregard these norms and taboos. The "eighteenth century" in Roth's formulation is a figure for a time when polymath intellectuals might write philosophy, novels, and political treatises as part of a single life's pursuit.

These Enlightenment figures are emblems of nonalienated intellectual labor, writers whom we imagine conducted their rich mental lives before modern rationalization carved out our contemporary landscape of disciplinary specialization, the division of labor, and so on. And as reviewers have frequently pointed out, DeWitt is as interested in writing fiction as she is in discussing information theory and linguistics and classical scholarship. One critic suggests that *The Last Samurai* is "a rare work of knowledge porn that actually conveys knowledge."[30] Unlike other recent novels such as *The Secret History* or *Special Topics in Calamity Physics*, the intellectual content of *The Last Samurai* "actually" matters to its author—and, by extension, is supposed to matter to us readers. What if, DeWitt seems to ask, our intellectual lives weren't so alienated? What if novels could produce and disseminate knowledge?

But as the conditional mood of these questions suggests, we seem not to live in such a world. A world where novels produce knowledge, where one's intellectual activity is fully integrated into one's life, is also sort of like a world where you can choose your own (good) father. That is, it's not ours. Our world, as reckoned by this standard, seems downright fallen, not unlike the unhappy modern world Georg Lukács describes in *The Theory of the Novel*. In such a world, there is a "rift between 'inside' and 'outside,'" an "essential difference between the self and the world, an incongruence between soul and deed."[31]

We might question such a claim about our divided life, but the lack of integrity of our world seems to be a postulate of DeWitt's literary imagination. And the motor of DeWitt's writing is, at its best, her will to represent and perhaps even try to reintegrate our damaged life, if only on the page. Yet the effort to have the novel be integrated into life runs into an intellectual and cultural division of labor that recognizes the novel in relation to a narrow domain of relevance. To write a novel that successfully demonstrates that reading Attic Greek is not so hard after all and that inspires readers on a mass scale to pick up Homer in the original requires that the different sort of world that such a novel aspires to make already exists. DeWitt's ambition to write a didactic novel, no less than to pick her own father, was in one sense doomed to fail from the beginning. But such a wish-fulfillment fantasy can still become the subject of a novel.

It is the subject of DeWitt's.

V

In her afterword to the New Directions edition of *The Last Samurai*, DeWitt writes that she was surprised to learn that some readers were impressed with Ludo's prodigious abilities. Why would they call the boy a genius when the evidence of the book offers no grounds for making such a judgment? "Since there is no age at which the opportunities offered Ludo are the norm," she observes, "we don't know whether he was a genius or not—only that he is an oddity in a society with very low expectations" (483). We live in a society, DeWitt suggests, dominated by the low expectations of people like Ludo's biological father, whom Sibylla mockingly calls Liberace. When Liberace meets Ludo for the first time, he is, like some (apparently misguided) readers of *The Last Samurai*, impressed by Ludo's abilities. Speaking of his other children (by a different mother), Liberace says that *Sesame Street* was "about the right level" for them at Ludo's age (277). The phrase disturbs the boy, haunting him, persuading him that his mother was right to conceal from him the identity of his father. A counterfactual life in which Ludo was raised by someone like Liberace seems unbearable. It would be a form of living death.

At an earlier moment in the novel, DeWitt offers another biting portrait of the low expectations of the society in which *The Last Samurai* was written. Sibylla often takes Ludo on London's Circle Line train to get away from their cold flat. Ludo brings along a range of texts to read on the Tube, a pushchair full, and he encounters many astonished riders who marvel at his ability to read the *Odyssey* in Greek. Over time, Sibylla conducts a "straw poll of Circle Line opinion on the subject of small children & Greek." Should small children be taught Attic Greek? Among the responses:

> Excellent idea as etymology so helpful for spelling: 19
> Excellent idea as inflected languages so helpful for computer programming: 8

Excellent idea as classics indispensable for understanding of English literature: 7

Excellent idea as Greek so helpful for reading New Testament, camel through eye of needle for example mistranslation of very similar word for rope: 3

(97)

These answers are contrasted with answers not given:

Marvellous idea as Homer so marvellous in Greek: o

Marvellous idea as Greek such a marvellous language: o

(98)

Sibylla indicts instrumental justifications for the study of Greek and presumably for learning more generally, suggesting that education is self-justifying and that mastering Greek, for example, ought to be regarded as an end in itself.

DeWitt is not indifferent to the worldly circumstances of education, and she does not mean to oppose art and commerce but to critique the current arrangement of education and commerce and to suggest what a rational set of institutional supports for art and learning might look like. Autotelic education requires, in her view, a radical transformation of our cultural institutions, social expectations, and economic lives. Only such widespread transformations would make serious study and true aesthetic appreciation possible. DeWitt's novel hopes for a world that might make it possible to write a better sort of literature and be ready to receive that literature. *The Last Samurai* is not an example of that hypothetical literature. DeWitt knows perfectly well—though she may not always admit it in interviews and essays—that such a vision of literature is, under current institutional arrangements, improbable. But the improbability of its own aspiration is part of what makes *The Last Samurai* compelling. As long as we live in a world of wasted potential, the book will continue to speak to those who might hope to build a better world, a more rational institutional life, and who hope art might play some role in the making of such a world.

2

HELEN DEWITT'S AESTHETIC EDUCATION

I

Helen DeWitt was a bored but dutiful child.[1] Her parents worked for
the Foreign Service, and though she was born in the United States, she
was raised abroad, moving from Mexico to Brazil to Columbia to Ecua-
dor, before returning as a teenager. Back in the States, she attended various boarding schools and Smith College. She came to find academic
life intolerable. "In America, especially, everything you do has to be con-
vertible, ultimately, into a credential," she lamented.[2] She didn't want a
credential. She wanted to lead a "life of the mind" but felt herself to be
surrounded everywhere by "intellectual mediocrity." After attempting
suicide at nineteen, DeWitt decided Oxford University might save her.
At Oxford, surely, she could live a life of intellectual freedom. She was
admitted, studied classics at Lady Margaret Hall, and received a senior
scholarship at Brasenose College, earning a DPhil in Greek and Latin
Literature in 1987.

Her dissertation was on the concept of propriety as a standard in
ancient literary criticism, and though she earned a fellowship to study
Arabic poetics, she decided not to stay in academia. She left partly
because she was unhappy with the realities of scholarly specialization
and partly because Oxford had not lived up to her expectations. "I was
trying to live by the standards of something that I had made up in my
head," she recalled, "a place where everyone had read Proust in French,
every classicist read the whole of Greek tragedy in the original."[3] Though

better than previous schooling experiences, Oxford proved not to be that place.

In *The Last Samurai*, Sibylla takes a similar intellectual path and suffers a similar disillusionment. Her parents, who own a motel chain, raise their (bored but brilliant) daughter in what Sibylla mockingly calls "Motelland" (23). We do not learn much about her life in the United States, though it's suggested that American life had become as intolerable for Sibylla as it seems to have been for DeWitt. Sibylla, too, we learn late in the novel, once attempted suicide. But when she (Sibylla) sees the film *A Yank at Oxford* (1938) on television, she decides to apply. And why not? "I could leave Motelland and live among rational beings!" she reports thinking. "I would never be bored again!" (23). Sibylla lies her way into Oxford but like DeWitt quickly discovers that her hopes were misplaced. Oxford proves to be something other than a citadel of reason. Here, Sibylla's story and DeWitt's diverge.

We can discern one rationale for Sibylla's departure in the story of Hugh Carey (HC) and Raymond Decker (RD), which she recounts to Ludo, presumably as a way of teaching the boy something about the character of the institution she abandoned. HC, we learn, arrives at Oxford at the precociously young age of fifteen but cynically treats his studies as a competitive game. He's primarily motivated by his competition with RD, the only person he thinks matches his intellect. RD is older but "largely self-taught" (321). Unlike HC, RD takes his studies so much to heart that he's paralyzed, barely able to take an exam because he cannot conceive what it would mean to reduce answers to complex philosophical questions into the short form required for written exams. HC must repeatedly persuade RD to take his exams. He does so by analogizing timed exam questions to fast chess. After being persuaded a few times, RD ultimately cannot go on. He fails to complete the *literae humaniores* degree because his examiner is "the finest Platonist of his generation and [has not published] for 20 years" (328).

In his exam book, RD writes, "I am not so presumptuous as to attempt in 40 minutes what Mr. JH has not achieved in 20 years," before deciding not to turn in his paper (328). Now having no competition, HC grows bored with the work of philology and leaves Oxford in search of living languages. Later in the novel, HC becomes a candidate father for Ludo and is tested by the boy. But when Sibylla first tells the story of RD and HC, the story is meant to reinforce the grounds of Sibylla's disenchantment, to suggest that Oxford enables the ambition of cynical strivers (HC) and fails to nurture those genuinely interested in learning (RD). The time when Oxford might welcome the finest (unpublished) Platonist of a generation has passed.

The proximate cause of Sibylla's decision to leave is, however, more specific. The pivotal moment of disillusionment comes when Sibylla reads a monograph by the German classical philologist Adolph Roemer, *Aristarchs Athetesen in der Homerkritik* (1912). Sibylla has lied about knowing German and so must laboriously make her way, with the aid of *Teach Yourself German*, through Roemer's book. What she finds in those pages shocks her. Roemer's monograph discusses the Homeric criticism of Aristarchus of Samothrace. Aristarchus was the librarian of the Library of Alexandria, a founding father of philology, and one of the great early critics of Homer. Though mostly lost, his criticism partly survives in the form of Iliadic scholia (marginal commentary on *The Iliad*). These scholia do not have names attached to them—so it's impossible to know which were written by Aristarchus—but Roemer makes confident pronouncements on which should be attributed to the great critic.

"Whenever someone else was said to have said something brilliant he [Roemer] saw instantly that it was really by Aristarchus, and if any brilliant comments happened to be lying around unclaimed he instantly spotted the unnamed mastermind behind them" (22). The problem with such an interpretation is not only that Roemer's motivated reasoning is, as Sibylla writes, "insane" but also that "Roemer had managed to write an entirely scholarly treatise without thinking for two seconds" (22). Roemer's unthinkingness comes, by a sort of transitive logic, to infect all the institutions that have taken him seriously. That is, for Sibylla, and perhaps DeWitt, it's one thing to be a shoddy or bad thinker. It is quite another, something rather worse, to celebrate and institutionalize shoddy or bad thought. Oxford is thus revealed to be bankrupt, only slightly better than the Motelland Sibylla left behind. It fails to live up to the standard Sibylla had expected it to uphold. Sibylla quits and takes up menial jobs because she would rather not return to the United States.

To be sure, DeWitt indicates that Sibylla likely has other reasons for leaving Oxford, reasons—we later realize, when Ludo's perspective enriches our understanding of his mother—that are related to her prior suicide attempt. It should also be noted that actual classicists are quite aware of these flaws in Roemer. As Francesca Schironi notes, Roemer's enthusiastic belief that "Aristarchus was always an excellent philologist according to *modern* standards" led the German critic to "distort the evidence at his disposal" when judging which scholia should be attributed to the Greek librarian.[4] But, in Sibylla's (admittedly self-serving) telling, it's Roemer's fallacious Homeric criticism that finally persuades her to leave Oxford and that sets in motion the sequence of events that will bring Ludo into the world.

It's appropriate, and no accident, that DeWitt stages Sibylla's disillusionment as an act of metacritical judgment (twice over). After all, Aristarchus's very name has come to be synonymous with criticism. To be an "Aristarch" is to be a severe critic. In critiquing Roemer, Sibylla asserts her critical superiority to a notable critic of a great critic of the greatest ancient poet. Sibylla's criticism of Roemer is thus both a declaration of filiation and the breaking of a genealogical line. Roemer joins the novel's long sequence of bad fathers who must be renounced before some new and better lineage can be discovered or created. And the German philologist's alignment with Oxford is meant to highlight how overcoming a bad father requires renouncing both individual bad men and the bad institutions that enable them.

The Last Samurai might, by this light, be viewed as a novel-length example of Quit Lit.[5] The genre typically features a narrative of academic breakdown and disillusionment. In the prototypical example of Quit Lit, we witness the journey of an Aspiring Academic who at first identifies wholly with the role, with the mission of higher education, and with the academic institutions that were once thought to sustain that mission. Enduring a series of abuses, humiliations, and travails, the Aspiring Academic discovers that academia is an uninhabitable planet, a discovery that sometimes requires a painful disidentification with a mentor or advisor to whom the Aspiring Academic has been complexly attached. Our hero will be forced to leave that destitute world, to discard the bad mentor. In this case, Sibylla's disillusionment (and DeWitt's) is structured around the clash of, on the one hand, the fantasy of Oxford as a home for reason and, on the other, the grubby ordinary reality of the place. In a final retrospective speech act, one that structures Quit Lit as a genre, our trusty narrator exposes the badness of the institution by ultimately affirming their own, higher rationality. The hero's act of public disavowal ultimately—dialectically—valorizes their intellectual seriousness, affirming the importance of the very values that the bad institution has failed to uphold or defend.

Sibylla "fritter[s] away her time" at Oxford "instead of advancing the frontiers of human knowledge" (17). She ultimately rejects her classical education. Yet the very act of impugning and abandoning that tradition, her very act of shirking, joins her to a distinguished lineage of Homeric criticism. If she's a lazy or bad student she's also, somehow, unusually well informed about, and deeply read in, the tradition she's rejecting. Sibylla, we are led to understand, is herself an Aristarch, the severest of severe critics.

II

Unlike Sibylla, DeWitt did successfully complete her degree. She won the prestigious Ireland Prize for young classicists and might have been able to make a career in the academy. Oxford University Press wanted to publish her dissertation. But DeWitt decided to leave. She didn't leave, or didn't only leave, because Oxford failed to live up to her fantastic standards. She also left because she discovered an alternative to the academic pursuit. In graduate school, she recalls, "a British Jew introduced me to Kurosawa and Sergio Leone and Dennis Potter, to the power of imaginary Americas."[6] That "British Jew" was David Levene, who was also completing a DPhil in classics at Oxford. They would be married for seven years. (He's now a professor at NYU.)

DeWitt characterizes the difference between Levene and her as a difference between radically different aesthetic preferences—between "spaghetti westerns, Mel Brooks, Wagner, Melville, Faulkner, Aeschylus" (his) and "Proust, Euripides" (hers).[7] DeWitt elaborates:

> David had this entirely different sensibility. He loves grand, mythic works of art. His favorite composer is Wagner. Among tragedians, he likes Aeschylus, whereas I'm a Euripides person. He introduced me to Sergio Leone and Kurosawa and Mel Brooks. The coexistence of these radically different aesthetic possibilities made me see ways that I could be a writer, things that I could do. He introduced me to bridge, to poker, to statistics, things that to other people might seem completely unrelated. . . . Previously I just thought, *What's the point in writing a novel? Everything's been done.* But now I saw, *No, there are so many things that have never been done! All these possibilities! This is so great!*[8]

Poker, bridge, statistics, Kurosawa, Mel Brooks: these are all topics DeWitt has written about. She tried to write a book about poker for Talk Miramax, and her second published novel, *Lightning Rods*, is a satire modeled on *The Producers*. So, by introducing her to Kurosawa, Levene clearly played a pivotal role in bringing *The Last Samurai* into the world.

However, the significance of DeWitt's encounter with Levene goes beyond her new appreciation for specific artworks and artists. What seems to have most enchanted DeWitt was not only the content of Levene's sensibility but also the possibility that other sensibilities might exist, that other aesthetic clusters—seemingly unrelated preferences—might coherently hang together. The encounter with aesthetic difference seems to have helped DeWitt recognize her own aesthetic preferences *as* preferences, to see that there were other artistic planets for her to explore, a whole universe of possibility. If the novel still had a mission in the closing years of the twentieth century, she might contribute something to its success.

An encounter with aesthetic difference is, of course, not guaranteed to expand one's imagination. Such an encounter might lead one not to appreciate new possibilities—*"All these possibilities!"*—but to double down on one's commitments. This is the outcome of Sibylla's encounter with

aesthetic difference. Her encounter with the travel writer Liberace—
whose sensibility is, to be sure, vastly different from hers—notably fails
to make her into a writer, and Ludo's later disappointing encounter with
his father is what inspires his quest to find alternative paternal role models. But though the major characters in *The Last Samurai* fail to have the
revelation that DeWitt describes herself as having had, DeWitt's bio-
graphical revelation nonetheless drives her novel. *The Last Samurai* is
structured around the pursuit of aesthetic education, the possibility of
educating oneself and honing a critical sensibility.

Halfway through the novel, Ludo confronts Sibylla in a scene that
especially highlights the stakes of this education. The boy, who has just
turned six, wants his mother to reveal to him the identity of his father.
All he knows is that his father is a travel writer. Over the course of several months, he tries with increasing desperation to convince her to reveal
his identity, and Sibylla finally responds by saying, "You will not be ready
to know your father until you can see what's wrong with these things"
(190). The "things" in question are works of art. One is a cassette featuring the music of the American pianist Liberace (not to be confused with
Ludo's father, Val Peters, whom Sibylla nicknames Liberace). The second is a postcard featuring the painting *Greek Girls Playing at Ball*, by
the Victorian painter Lord Fredric Leighton. The third is a magazine
article by an unnamed American writer.

Exasperated, Ludo asks Sibylla to just tell him what's wrong with
these works. "I won't say it's better for you to work it out for yourself,"
his mother responds, "le formule est banale" (190–91). Then she adds a
warning: "Even when you see what's wrong you won't really be ready.
You should not know your father [even] when you have learnt to despise
the people who made these things. Perhaps it would be all right when
you have learnt to pity them, or if there is some state of grace beyond
pity when you have reached that state" (191). Why are these works bad?
And what does Ludo's recognizing their badness have to do with his
readiness to meet his father?

Earlier in the novel, we get a few hints. Sibylla has described Liberace (the musician) as having "a terrible facility and a terrible sincerity;

what he played he played with feeling" (54). Liberace's style of kitsch can also be found in the writing of Ludo's father; they share a certain "emotional facility" (55). The boy's father's writing exhibits "the slick buttery arpeggios, the self-regarding virtuosity as the clever ring-laden hands sparkled over the keys, the professional sincerity which found expressiveness for the cynical & the sentimental, for the pornographic, even for alienation & affectlessness" (55). Unlike the musician Liberace, however, Ludo's father lacks "technical facility" (55). The travel writer shows himself, again and again, to be "innocent of logic in all his written work" and is no better in person (64). Here's a man who, Sibylla observes, "learned to write before he could think, a man who threw out logical fallacies like tracks behind a getaway car, and he always always always got away" (56).

The Victorian painter Lord Leighton is criticized on similar grounds. His "masterly use of perspective," in Sibylla's view, is "shallow and superficial and even artless" when compared to a print by the Japanese woodblock artist Utamaro (59–60). "Lord Leighton" is also Sibylla's nickname for an American writer whom Liberace admires (the writer of the magazine article). This author writes in "a gorgeous train of sentences swathing his poor stupid thoughts" (67). The breathless vapidity of Lord Leighton (the writer) is evident in the tiniest gestures of his characters, which are freighted with meaning, but a sort of meaning that is finally empty. His prose proffers false beauty. Something similar, we are led to believe, might be said for Lord Leighton (the painter), whose *Greek Girls Playing at Ball* Ludo has been asked to judge. Sibylla explains that "it is the faultlessness of [Lord Leighton's] skill which makes the paintings embarrassing to watch, so bare do they strip the mind of their creator" (67).

As for the writer of the magazine article—the American writer Sibylla nicknames Lord Leighton—we don't learn much about him, beyond the fact that Ludo's father is (of course) a fan. Years later, the writer publishes a novel. Now almost eleven, Ludo informs his mother, "According to one reviewer this writer I am supposed to regard from a state of grace beyond pity is the greatest writer in English in the world today. . . . Nine out of ten reviewers gave him a rating of 'great' or better" (230). Sibylla replies, "Anything follows from a false premise" (230).

After another exasperating conversation, Ludo concludes that "what's bad about these people is that they are bad artists. Maybe my father was a bad writer—but it could be because he had more important things to think about. . . . Sibylla does tend to take art too seriously" (233).

Too seriously, indeed. For Sibylla, aesthetic judgment, no less than critical judgment, bears a grave moral dimension. What is at stake when judging art is, on this view, not only whether a work is good or bad but also what its goodness or badness reveals about the character of the person who made it. Nicknaming Ludo's father Liberace tells us everything we need to know about the man. The kitschy artwork can only be made by the kitschy soul, and the pianist Liberace, the painter Lord Leighton, and the American writer all exhibit a terrible kitschy sincerity, made manifest in a slickly, elegant, buttery artistic style, which exposes their fundamental sentimentality and the shoddiness of their thought. Their sincerity is, ultimately, precritical.

Worse, they make their art in a society that lets them get away with badness, that celebrates them for it. In such a world, critics—"nine out of ten"—cannot be trusted. This is how, as the critic and novelist Jenny Davidson has suggested, style for DeWitt becomes "the repository of character, something we have an obligation to judge: to judge, and to cry out against when we find it wanting."[9] Sibylla hopes that Ludo might be able to bypass his own bad (biological) father and proceed straight to a better life; she hopes that the male figures in Kurosawa's *Seven Samurai* might serve as adequate masculine role models. But before he can do so he will have to learn to identify and reject bad art. Before he can understand the inadequacy of his father, that is, Ludo will need to learn to read the moral significance of style.

Sibylla's judgments are often disproportionate and cruel, but the command to cultivate one's aesthetic sensibility is also clearly directed at the reader of *The Last Samurai*. Like Ludo, we are put on trial, are asked to develop our ability to see the connection between style and character, are instructed to take art "too seriously." *The Last Samurai*'s mode of persuasion isn't only to make a philosophical case that literature should move beyond existing limitations and that artists should embrace modernist seriousness again. *The Last Samurai* also indirectly enacts its vision of a more advanced literature on the page, trying to show how and why our personal standards are inadequate, indicting existing literary institutions, practices, and norms.

DeWitt prosecutes her case by focusing her attention—and ours—on the limitations of our time, making us aware of the degree to which we have been asked to lower our standards and squander our potential. The account of this alternative art can seem, at times, unforgivingly stringent—Liberace doesn't really seem that bad, now, does he?—and it should be said that *The Last Samurai* does not straightforwardly embody its own theories of achieved art, but the novel nonetheless invites the reader to adopt a new critical stance from which they'll be able to appreciate DeWitt's aspiration. We're asked to imagine that how we interpret art reveals something about our worthiness or virtue and shows us the degree to which we move purposively or unthinkingly through life.

DeWitt's great subject, here and across her writing, is what most people fail to think about—norms, habits, and institutions they take as given. *The Last Samurai* aims to expose these given standards, to analyze the operation of such standards, and to contribute to the construction of better standards (and norms and institutions). "The fact is," Sibylla complains, "that 99 out of 100 adults spare themselves the trouble of rational thought 99% of the time (studies have not shown this, I have just invented the statistics so I should say not The fact is, but I would be surprised if the true figures were very different)" (68). We're asked to see, in Sibylla's uncompromising stance, the harsh—but also hilarious and joyous—possibility that things might be otherwise. We're asked to expand the range of our imaginations, to open ourselves to possibilities we might otherwise have imagined to be out of reach, to think, as DeWitt once did, *"No, there are so many things that have never been done! All these possibilities! This is so great!"*

This is the critical power of art.

III

The Last Samurai does not only condemn the bad example of Liberace. It also develops an alternative, better vision of what art might aspire to be. Early in the novel, Sibylla describes her enthusiasm for Arnold Schoenberg's *Theory of Harmony*, and she espouses latter-day modernist schemes for how a future literature might absorb Schoenberg's insights on musical composition. Schoenberg, who published his *Harmonielehre* in 1911, is held up as a rational—and moral—counterpoint to Roemer's illogic. While Schoenberg is "scraping a living as a teacher of music & portrait painter," Roemer is peddling his studied nonsense from a comfortable sinecure at the University of Leipzig (58). Schoenberg is a candidate good father for Sibylla, over and against Roemer's badness.

What does this better alternative look like?

Sibylla is particularly taken with Schoenberg's argument about dissonance and cites his claim that it's the destiny of music to exploit all the elements "latent in sound." Her reverie after encountering Schoenberg leads her to riff on what a future literature might attempt:

> It seemed to me reading Schoenberg that what the writers of the future would do was not necessarily say: I am writing about an Armenian grandfather Czech grandmother a young biker from Kansas (of Czech & Armenian descent), Armenian Czech English OK. Gradually they would approach the level of the other branches of the arts which are so much further developed. Perhaps a writer would think of the monosyllables and lack of grammatical inflection in Chinese, and of how this would sound next to lovely long Finnish words all double letters & long vowels in 14 cases or lovely Hungarian all prefixes suffixes, & having first thought of that would then think of some story about Hungarians or Finns with Chinese.
>
> (60–61)

It's the job of the ambitious artist, Sibylla suggests, to activate previously latent facets of language, facets that go beyond invoking the referential function of sentences and that showcase the possibility of a pure play of phonemes and lexemes, the delightful properties of Chinese inflections, Hungarian prefixes and suffixes, and so on. Such a writer would develop a storyline retroactively, only after making an initial decision to play with certain textual possibilities.

This definition of the purpose of art sounds familiar, resembling in some ways the Russian formalist description of art as an engine of defamiliarization. "Defamiliarization," or *ostranenie*—alternately translated as "estrangement"—is a concept most associated with the founding father of formalism, the critic and novelist Viktor Shklovsky. "The purpose of art," Shklovsky writes in a classic 1917 essay, "is to lead us to knowledge of a thing through the organ of sight instead of recognition."[10] Art takes familiar objects, which through long exposure become subject to "automized perception," and makes us *see* those objects again. It systematically defeats the habituated oblivion most of us inhabit most of the time.

In highlighting habituation, the concept of *ostranenie* doesn't only give an account of art's relation to human perception. It also posits a theory of art's relationship to itself, an explanation of the driving force of artistic change. When devices become canonized, too familiar, cliché, they lose their ability to revivify the world. Artists hoping to create living art must therefore develop new devices. And so, art moves on, is forced to change, and (in a narrowly defined sense) progresses. This account of art, consilient with modernist and avant-garde ideas of artistic innovation, encodes a set of assumptions about how an idealized—and homogeneous—modern readership comes to internalize specific expectations about art and then (repeatedly) should have those expectations shattered.

Sibylla's drive to "strike a style to amaze," no less than her reverence for Schoenberg, seems to put her in a decidedly modernist camp (31). And her emphasis on the purely formal features of language might lead some readers to worry that she and perhaps DeWitt, too, devalue literary self-expression or identity-oriented forms of writing. Sibylla's aesthetic commitments might seem, from this vantage point, curiously apolitical. But there are key features of Sibylla's ambition that separate her (and DeWitt) from modernism, and her turn to linguistic form, I'd argue, also has a particular political content in the closing years of the twentieth century. DeWitt's differences with modernism become clearer when we examine her training as a classicist and read her dissertation, which she completed in 1987. The dissertation, called "Quo Virtus? The Concept of Propriety in Ancient Literary Criticism" is a survey of the concept of propriety in Greek and Latin literary criticism. Its account of propriety is complicated, surveying quite different versions of the concept.

"Propriety" names a range of overlapping concepts, from "the idea that elevated subjects called for elevated language to the idea that heroes should not be made to seem cowardly."[11] Propriety is, in short, an aesthetic canon of plausibility and decorum, speaking to what is likely to happen under specified circumstances or designating what ought to be said about certain types of character. It will just not do to represent a king as base, for example, because even if actual kings behaved badly, it would be untoward to represent them this way. At root, propriety is the adherence to an established social norm or standard. To promote propriety as a standard is, in a sense, to offer a metanorm, one that argues for the value of hewing to what is done because it's what's done. The challenge of upholding such a metastandard is coming up with a rationale for propriety in the face of audiences who seem to like the wrong kind of art. DeWitt asks: "Can criteria for artistic excellence be found which are independent of what people happen to like, and which can therefore justify claims about what they should like? Second, where does use of the concept place ancient literary discussion in relation to various forms of modern literary theory and criticism?"[12] DeWitt's dissertation offers a wide-ranging set of answers to these questions, exploring how different critics deployed different senses of propriety, how they thought about the taste of disparate audiences, and how they conceptualized correctness.

Her survey leads her to conclude that the ancient concept might be less useful to *modern critics* than to *modern writers*. Thinking about propriety, she writes (in an epilogue she physically appended to the dissertation after it was submitted), "raises questions . . . about the blind spots in works of literature as they are written today—about the artificial limitations which continue to be taken as natural, and the constraints on the kinds of difficulty works of literature are allowed to present." Her main illustration of an artificial limitation is directly relevant to *The Last Samurai* and bears a resemblance to Sibylla's Schoenberg-inspired imagined future for literature. DeWitt chides a literature that fails to present "foreigners as articulate speakers of their own languages." Such a presentation assumes that, for example, the American novel ought to be a novel written in English. But why not write novels that include multiple languages? There are "commercial difficulties" that prevent American authors from publishing multilingual works, but other significant barriers are the commonplace cultural assumptions about what literature should do. If the difficulty were only commercial, we might expect "large numbers of manuscripts passed from hand to hand, and to hear a good deal of debate about the possibilities of the form." Instead, there is only "resounding silence."[13]

We can now see the gap between DeWitt and formalism.[14] DeWitt is not much concerned with art's effect on the habituated consciousness of a hypothetical general reader, nor does she develop new artistic devices through which to render lost objects again visible. She is, in one sense, indifferent to the consciousness of her audience, though not in the way some critics celebrate as a hallmark of modernism.[15] Likewise, she's not obsessed with the internal relations of literary form and the autonomy of art (quite the opposite in fact, since she often speaks of art in instrumental terms). Instead, DeWitt focuses on the normative social standards and aesthetic horizons within which artists work and within which readers read. DeWitt is interested in what artists take for granted, what they assume they are and aren't allowed to do or say, and the institutions that hem in what they can say. She asks the American novel of the late twentieth century to be more ambitious, to discard its Anglocentrism, and to widen its geographic and linguistic horizons. She asks something similar of the reader. After all, the *ambitious writer* of the future—who loves the "monosyllables and lack of grammatical inflection in Chinese," "lovely long Finnish words all double letters & long vowels in 14 cases," and "lovely Hungarian all prefixes suffixes"—will require a corresponding *ambitious reader*, one who might judge such a virtuosic textual performance. DeWitt's vision of art is political to the degree that making the polyglot literary world she dreams of anything more than a quixotic fantasy would require a wholesale transformation of many existing norms and institutions.

The voice of repressive normative standards is dramatized within *The Last Samurai* in the voice of a quasi-character called "the Alien." The Alien first speaks to Sibylla when Ludo asks her if he can learn the Greek alphabet:

> And now the Alien spoke, & its voice was mild as milk. It said: He's just a baby. They spend so much time in school—wouldn't he be better off playing?
>
> I said: Let him wait to be bored in a class like everyone else.
>
> The Alien said: It will only confuse him! It will destroy his confidence! It would be kinder to say no!
>
> The Alien has a long eel-like neck and little reptilian eyes. I put both hands around its throat & I said: Rot in hell.
>
> It coughed & said sweetly: So sorry to intrude. Admirable maternity! All time devoted to infant amelioration. Selflessly devoted!
>
> I said: Shut up.
>
> It said: Sssssssssssssssssssssssssssss.
>
> I said: Grrrrrrrrrrrrrrrrrrrrrrrrrrrrr.
>
> (45–46)

The Alien repeatedly tells Sibylla that Ludo is "only four" and need not be taught Greek at such a young age (46). When Sibylla is tempted to introduce Ludo to Liberace, the temptation comes to her in the form of the voice of the Alien. "The Alien whispered He's not a bad man." And: "The Alien whispered It's only fair to give the other side a chance" (76). We later learn that the Alien is "whatever you want to call the thing that finds specious reasons for cruelty" (100). "Give the other side a fair chance" is, in a sense, the negative slogan of the novel (the counterpoint to "a good samurai will parry the blow"). The phrase embodies the sort of rationalizations that can lead people to waste their potential. It incarnates conventional wisdom.

The Alien also arguably makes a silent appearance at other moments in the text when Sibylla confronts the conventional expectations of parenthood. For example, at one point in the novel Ludo decides to stay out all night in his pursuit of the Egyptian-Hungarian adventurer, pseudo-diplomat, and gambler Mustafa Szegeti, one of the candidate fathers he has selected. The boy calls to tell his mother that he's not coming home. "Sibylla did not say anything for a very long time," Ludo tells us. "I knew what she was thinking anyway. The silence stretched out, for my mother was debating inwardly the right of one rational being to exercise arbitrary authority over another rational being on the ground of seniority. Or rather she was not debating this, for she did not believe in such a right, but she was resisting the temptation to exercise such power sanctioned only by the custom of the day" (408).

J. S. Mill excluded children from the circle of those who are due liberty, but Sibylla adheres to a more capacious understanding of human autonomy, one that includes very young children. The parent-child relationship should—in its ideal form, a form Sibylla hopes to uphold—be governed by the mutual recognition of rational choice. Rational authority, the authority of knowledge and expertise, is affirmed over and against arbitrary authority. Yet the reader is surely supposed to share Sibylla's hesitation at this moment. We're tempted to wish she would exercise arbitrary authority over Ludo, before coming to recognize and reject the Alien's voice within ourselves.

The phrase "give the other side a chance" is the same phrase Sibylla's paternal grandfather uses to persuade Sibylla's father not to attend Harvard at the age of fifteen. When Sibylla's father is admitted, he tells his father, and, Sibylla writes, "Something looked through my grandfather's beautiful eyes. Something spoke with his beautiful voice, and it said: 'It's only fair to give the other side [i.e., the side of religious education] a chance'" (3). Sibylla's father's choice to attend a seminary will prove fatal, leave him stranded running a chain of motels, creating the Motelland Sibylla will come to find unbearable. Sibylla's uncle Buddy, too, confronts his own version of the Alien when he's contemplating his future. Buddy wants to be an opera singer, but his father (Sibylla's maternal grandfather) insists that he train instead as an accountant, and at one point in the narrative "something" looks through the eyes of Buddy's father and says, "Being an accountant, it's not the end of the world" (79). The Alien is thus embodied in specific parental figures (both of Sibylla's grandfathers), yet even for these characters, when we look closer, the Alien is a malign force operating within them that arrests or corrupts their full agency. The Alien seems to be nothing other than introjected social norms, and no less than either of her grandfathers, Sibylla discovers her own inner Alien. The difference between her and her grandfathers is that Sibylla recognizes the inner Alien *as* an Alien. When the Alien tells her that teaching Greek to Ludo would be a bad idea, Sibylla doesn't go along with the Alien's soothing suggestions. After all, her own life would be much easier if she listened to the Alien and didn't give in to Ludo's nagging. Sibylla fights the Alien and fatefully decides to begin the long process of teaching Ludo—and by extension, the reader—the Greek alphabet, writing out a table of Greek letters for the boy.

Grrrrrrrrrrrrrrrrrrrrrrrrrr.

It's therefore against *artificial limitation*, not *automized perception*, that DeWitt directs her criticism. Artificial limitations can be internalized as norms of propriety, but they can also be embodied in social institutions and cultural practices. In an interview, DeWitt once suggested that "if we could send a photocopier back to 5th-century Athens by time machine, we could have all too of Sophocles' plays instead of 7; if we sent it along with *the sociological structures* in which the machine is now embedded, we would be lucky to get 7."[16] Sociological structures such as the contemporary publishing field put barriers between authors and audiences, leave potential classics behind. Editors might do better if they exercised *less* oversight.

We have reason to be skeptical of such a claim. DeWitt should, at the very least, recognize that there were myriad "sociological structures" shaping what Sophocles could and could not do, and there's no guarantee that the rest of Sophocles's plays would be of artistic interest. Whatever we think about DeWitt's argument in this specific case, her fiction is about making normative standards visible *as standards*. Ancient critics engaged in a kind of metanormative criticism that argued one should do what was proper because it was proper; today, writers, critics, and readers do the same but often don't even realize they're doing it. DeWitt wants to hold what is taken to be proper to a higher standard of scrutiny. And in trying to develop this higher standard, DeWitt is forced to

A	B	Γ	Δ	E	Z	H	Θ	I	K	Λ	M
A	B	G	D	E	Z	Ē	TH	I	K	L	M

α	β	γ	δ	ε	ζ	η	θ	ι	κ	λ	μ
a	b	g	d	e	z	ē	th	i	k	l	m

N	Ξ	O	Π	P	Σ	T	Y	Φ	X	Ψ	Ω
N	X	O	P	R	S	T	U	PH	KH	PS	Ō

ν	ξ	ο	π	ρ	σ,ς	τ	υ	φ	χ	ψ	ω
n	x	o	p	r	s	t	u	ph	kh	ps	ō

Sibylla's table of Greek letters.

aim her criticism against social institutions that, whether they know it or not, bear responsibility for deciding what is and isn't done. Her fiction is obsessed with what is absent from contemporary literature; it anatomizes taken-for-granted forms of reasoning and canons of probability that define conventional novelistic prose.

Ultimately, DeWitt calls for a contemporary literary culture that is conscious that it is constricted by unacknowledged ideas of propriety. She seeks to create a literature that overcomes those assumed limits. If we read *The Last Samurai* through the aesthetic category of propriety, we can learn much about DeWitt's vision of art. What becomes visible, on the one hand, is the need for an enlarged understanding of what art is and what it might become and, on the other, a renewed focus on the relation of art to its grounding "sociological structures."

But, of course, *The Last Samurai* would not be in our hands today if it didn't itself pass through the sieve of our own contemporary "sociological structures," which, on the one hand, constituted one important condition of possibility of its publication and, on the other, became the indirect subject of the book. Trained in classics at Oxford, an expert in the ancient critical category of "propriety," aspiring to bring ambitious new possibilities into the ambit of the experimental or difficult American novel, DeWitt was given her chance. After a torturous process of composition, her novel would win a high-profile publishing contract.

All she'd have to do was get the book into print.

3

SYNERGY IS CRAP

I

Jonathan Burnham moved from London to New York City in 1998. After five years as publishing director of Chatto & Windus, an imprint of Random House UK, he came to the United States to work as senior editor at Viking Penguin.[1] But he didn't stay long in the position. Through a friend, he was introduced to Tina Brown. Brown was leaving her position as editor of the *New Yorker* to start a new company, Talk Media, which would be a magazine, a book publisher, and possibly a television studio connected to Miramax Films. Brown had tried but failed to create a similar multimedia venture at the *New Yorker*; now she had a chance to realize her vision with the backing of Bob and Harvey Weinstein. *Talk* was meant to be a "reinvention of the upscale general interest magazine."[2] Burnham met with the Weinstein brothers and was offered the positions of president and editor in chief of Talk Miramax Books and literary editor of *Talk* magazine.

Miramax had already been publishing books, but most were related to film properties. Miramax Books had, for example, published screenplays by Quentin Tarantino. Now, the Weinstein brothers wanted to publish books that would synergize with their other properties. "We can find a way to create a one-hour television special around a brilliant non-fiction piece, or it could become the basis of . . . movies," Harvey Weinstein explained. "It's all about content."[3] Burnham took the job on the condition that he could create his own list, though he agreed that his list would partly be fed by work published in the magazine and projects Miramax was pursuing. This commitment did not seem too onerous because, as Burnham explained, Miramax was in its heyday "one of the most literary" of the independent film houses.[4]

Talk magazine turned into a high-profile bust. Brown burned through fifty million dollars, running the magazine into the ground.[5] But the book division, helmed by Burnham, was described by the *New York Times*, among others, as a "rare success" and was pointed to "as proof of the synergies in their marriage of [Weinstein's] film company and [Brown's] knowledge of publishing."[6] Burnham had money to spend on big acquisitions but was running a lean office, with only a handful of people directly on staff. As a publisher without a backlist, Talk Miramax had to aggressively pursue acquisitions, paying upward of $3 million for Rudy Giuliani's memoir and fighting at auction for the rights to Rick Riordan's *Percy Jackson and the Olympians*. Burnham explained the success of his new venture by saying, "That tired word 'synergy' actually does come into effect with the way we work. . . . I can buy a project, a book, which they can develop as a movie or they can discover a script, which I can turn into a book."[7]

"Synergy" is a name for the hope that firms from different industries might be more profitable in combination, that a conglomerate might be more valuable than the sum of its parts. In the 1990s, there was a wave of mergers and acquisitions (M&A) across media-related industries, often justified as a pursuit of synergy, but there was also a growing critique of the economic irrationality of the mania for consolidation.[8] Indeed, the term "synergy" came to be roundly mocked. S. I. Newhouse Jr., the owner of Advance Publications, once quipped that "synergy is crap" after the promised synergies of acquiring Random House failed to materialize, and Advance Publications decided to sell Random House to Bertelsmann A.G. in 1998 for $1.4 billion.[9] Even so, the promise of synergy remained seductive. Synergy might be viewed as a capitalist form of magical thinking, a dream that the commixture of different properties might spontaneously produce economic value, as if from nothing, by removing friction from the process of profit generation. We should, therefore, take the concept of "synergy" seriously—if not as a theory of the benefits of agglomeration, then as a corporate fantasy with real consequences.

Synergy may, indeed, be crap from the perspective of profitability, but our mediasphere is nonetheless littered with the luminescent turds produced in the wake of such irrational optimism. Corporate firms don't always do what's in their own best interests, and their failure to do what's in a larger sense economically rational is arguably intrinsic to their status as capitalist firms. At minimum, we might agree that the pursuit of synergy has changed the circumstances of contemporary authorship and has had aesthetic effects. As Henry Jenkins argues, synergy is not synonymous with merchandizing and licensing. Under the paradigm of synergy, licensing gives way to "co-creation," in which "companies collaborate from the beginning to create content they know plays well in each of their sectors, allowing each medium to generate new experiences for the consumer and expand the points of entry into the franchise."[10] Jenkins has in mind multimodal franchises like *The Matrix* (which told its story not only in films but also in video games and animated shorts). Individual artists become, on this model, more and more subsumed into forms of corporate authorship.

We might ask what "synergy" or "co-creation" means when writing and publishing a novel, which seems harder to assimilate to this aesthetic paradigm.[11] To be sure, DeWitt did not have any interest in creating a synergistic transmedia franchise, and Talk Miramax was not an acquisition but an entirely new business. Yet the M&A wave in the 1990s, and the attendant dream of synergy, was an important context for Burnham's acquisition of *The Last Samurai*. As I mentioned in chapter 1, Burnham first read the manuscript that would become *Lightning Rods* and initially passed on it; next he read what at that point was still called "The Seventh Samurai" and, as one does, fell in love. It's easy to guess why he would have preferred *The Last Samurai* to *Lighting Rods*. *Lightning Rods* is a deeply strange satire of corporate feminism, in which a vacuum cleaner salesman named Joe creates an improbably successful company that hires out sex workers who pretend to be ordinary temp workers—who surreptitiously provide sexual services to "high-performing" employees using an elaborate contraption in office bathrooms. (It's complicated!)

By contrast, *The Last Samurai* can, for all its complexity, seem more conventional, especially when the formal difficulty of Sibylla's half of the novel gives way to Ludo's linear, fable-like quest.[12] DeWitt recalled that Burnham described the book to her as a "love story between a mother and a son."[13] Others share Burnham's view. Edward Mendelson, in his *New York Review of Books* review, suggests that the novel is ultimately about "the nature and efficacy of human love."[14] This is an eminently plausible reading, but DeWitt didn't see her novel that way. She thought of it, instead, as a book about a mother's anguish at having to make sacrifices to protect her child, less a love story than a story about the terrible cost of love.

We might ask an obvious question: Did Jonathan Burnham acquire *The Last Samurai* based on a misreading? DeWitt would probably say he did. But as DeWitt herself recognizes, the "sociological structures" of contemporary publishing, which take manuscripts and consecrate them as books, are highly opinionated—and take a toll on (or from) works they ferry into the world. Today, myriad self-publishing platforms exist, and DeWitt has been an early adopter of these platforms, self-publishing her coauthored novel *Your Name Here* on her website as a PDF, making it possible for readers to pay her directly via PayPal. Yet in 1998, when she finally sold the manuscript of "The Seventh Samurai," fewer self-publishing options were available. DeWitt ultimately needed to sell her book to an editor if she wanted to find a readership. And to seek publication is, perhaps inevitably, to seek to be misread. After all, from the moment a manuscript dreams of becoming a book, it encounters a range of intermediaries, each of whom is empowered by and constrained by specific "sociological structures" to decide its fate.

II

Many sociologists and scholars of contemporary literature have written about these structures. The most complete account of the contemporary publishing process in the United States is Clayton Childress's analysis of the publication of a single novel—Cornelia Nixon's *Jarrettsville*—from creation through reception. Modifying concepts drawn from Pierre Bourdieu, Childress describes the making of Nixon's book in terms of three interacting fields. Each of these fields is a "field" in a technical sense. The term "field" names a structured set of rules and norms, organized around different kinds of "capital," which define a range of moves available to players. Fields are competitive spaces where players vie for dominant positions, making moves dictated by a set of rules and according to a set of values specific to that field. The point of describing a field as a "field" is that the players who participate in a field don't openly compete for economic resources. Each field enjoys relative autonomy, in the sense that it largely legislates its own activities, judging these activities in terms of local rules, habits, norms, and objectives.

In Childress's model of publishing, the "field of creation" encompasses the world of the author. Along with the author's immediate collaborators and first readers, we might include MFA programs, writing groups, and an author's friends and family. DeWitt did not earn an MFA, though she was very much a product of the academy, a long-term resident of institutions of higher education, albeit a very uneasy resident of these institutions, which partly accounts for what makes *The Last Samurai* unique. Nor did DeWitt come to writing through journalism or through employment in a major culture industry center, though she did live in London when she was writing the novel. In the field of creation as it was constituted for her, we can include DeWitt and her ex-husband David Levene, who was involved in the creation of *The Last Samurai*, as well as Maude Chilton and Tim Schmidt, who read early drafts of the book. The field of creation, Childress argues, speaks "the language of art." That is, it values a piece of writing in terms of an aesthetic vocabulary. Next comes the "field of production," the universe of middlemen who represent, acquire, sell, and produce manuscripts. For *The Last Samurai*, this second field might encompass Stephanie Cabot, Rebecca Wilson, Jonathan Burnham, everyone who worked at Talk Miramax Books, and the two dozen international editors who snapped up the rights to translate *The Last Samurai* at the Frankfurt Book Fair in 1999. The field of production, Childress argues, speaks a "language of commerce." It's focused on the prospects for turning a work of art into a salable commodity.

Finally, we arrive at the "field of circulation," which encompasses individual readers, book clubs, scholars, and others who frame and interpret the book. In this field, the language of valuation (and evaluation) is a "language of meaning." A book is assessed for what new perspectives and insights it can offer to readers.

Each field operates according to its own logic, yet manuscripts also must be "pitched" from one field to another before they can become books. Certain players—agents, book buyers, reviewers—act as intermediaries, translating the value of the underlying manuscript from the language of one field into the language of another. This is the sense in which the three fields "operate both independently and interdependently."[15] The strength of Childress's model is that it can explain the operations of the literary field without reducing it to a mechanistic process and without robbing artists, editors, or readers of agency. Literary critics are sometimes allergic to sociological methods, assuming those methods reduce the complexity of literary life or impose simplistic structural explanations upon literary outcomes. But the work of great literary sociologists such as Childress, Wendy Griswold, and John Thompson belie such easy dismissal. Instead, their important scholarship maps the relation between structure and agency without reducing one to the other. Authors write their own literature, but they do not write it under self-selected circumstances.

Interpreted by the light of such models, *The Last Samurai* might be said to align with Talk Miramax's commitment to synergy as a corporate strategy, albeit indirectly. After all, Miramax Films won its first Best Picture Oscar in 1997 for its adaptation of Michael Ondaatje's novel *The English Patient*. The film option to DeWitt's book had already been sold before Talk Miramax acquired it, but the manuscript's extensive intertextual dialogue with Kurosawa's *Seven Samurai* undoubtedly suggested the possibility of converting a literary property into an Oscar-worthy Indiewood hit. And for a publisher hoping to build a strong front list, the opportunity to have first dibs on future writing by DeWitt was surely tantalizing. Yet the story of *The Last Samurai* also highlights weaknesses in Childress's model, which, in my view, keeps its three interdependent fields too far from one another. To be clear, the problem isn't exactly that

Childress reduces the agency of the author or the editor or the reader, in favor of structural, mechanistic, or monocausal explanations for their behavior. Rather, I'd argue that Childress and similar field models can be too rigorous in their account of the division of labor between different players of a particular field. At times, we end up with an *insufficiently mechanistic* account of why certain players at specific field-positions behave the way they do.

That is, it's not only intermediary figures—like agents—who move between fields; every actor at every point in the field also often engages in acts of translating between registers of value. If Burnham and DeWitt interpreted the novel—back when it was still called "The Seventh Samurai"—differently, it wasn't only because author and editor inhabit different fields, which embody different vocabularies of value, but also because Burnham had a different aesthetic sensibility than DeWitt—a rival sensibility. He acquired the book based on an interpretation of the book that differed from the author's, an interpretation that also surely anticipated the way the book would be received in the field of circulation. On this view, if the novel was a successful work of art, it was successful despite DeWitt's intention. Whether or not we agree with Burnham's interpretation, my point is that the acquisitions process is never only a commercial act. It is also, and always, an act of aesthetic judgment.[16] To be sure, Burnham wanted to strengthen the market position of Talk Miramax. But doing so would require more than acquiring bestsellers. As a brand associated with "quality indies," Talk Miramax would build its reputation, at least in part, on its demonstrated good taste. The languages of art, commerce, and meaning coexist everywhere, at every position, in the fields Childress describes.

It would correspondingly be a mistake to claim that DeWitt was solely invested in her novel's status as art—and disinterested in commerce or meaning. While Talk Miramax's dreams of synergy might partly help explain Burnham's acquisition of *The Last Samurai*, those dreams also provide the background against which DeWitt wrote, edited, and promoted her book. And as we have already seen, DeWitt is nothing if not obsessed with the relationship between commerce and art. She alternates between condemning existing commercial institutions and imagining more effective—if also fantastical—versions of those institutions. Her fictions feature many artists and artist-like figures who face the art world's institutional players—literary agents, gallery owners, editors, patrons—and who dream of participating in more rational institutions. The character of Joe in *Lighting Rods* is, after all, a successful entrepreneur, someone who finds a way to turn his bizarre sexual fantasies and his internalization of the discourse of self-help into a wildly profitable company.

Sometimes it's the author who aspires to be the ruthlessly efficient profit maximizer. And in a world that increasingly asks authors to think of themselves as brand names or "entrepreneurs of the self," she increasingly must take on this role herself, participating in the destruction of certain features of the relative autonomy she may previously have enjoyed.[17] Yet even within the heart of corporate decision making, which might seem antithetical to art or literature, aesthetic judgments nonetheless persist.[18] That is, entrepreneurs of the self cannot avoid making aesthetic judgments.

The Last Samurai is no less interested in commerce than *Lightning Rods*. Indeed, studying how the novel anticipates its own transition from the field of creation to the field of production, how it forcefully critiques meddlesome middlemen, can offer us (twenty years later, way over here in the field of reception) a better handle on the book. It might also give us a way of thinking about what it would mean for a novel, written by an individual author, to be a corporate "co-creation."

III

After all, might *The Last Samurai* not be regarded as a novel about the promise and failure of corporate synergy? Is Ludo anything other than the child of the "conglomerate era" in publishing?[19] The unpleasant one-night stand between Sibylla and Liberace that produces Ludo is not only a meeting between two human persons but also a literary event. I have already described the union as a confrontation between two rival sensibilities, and I have already suggested that for Sibylla, Liberace's aesthetic deficiencies have an ineradicably moral dimension. These deficiencies indict not only Liberace but the social, economic, and literary world that celebrates and empowers the likes of him.

But let's recall that Sibylla and Liberace's misbegotten hookup is also the product of a corporate merger. Around the time she meets Ludo's father, Sibylla is working as a secretary for a "small publishing house in London" that specializes "in dictionaries and non-academic works of scholarship" (49). When her small imprint is acquired by a "big American company," the small imprint is assured that it will remain "autonomous," which is taken as evidence by the staff that "everyone would soon be redundant" (54).

The merger provides the occasion for a party to celebrate the corporate marriage, and one of the American publisher's big authors, the writer Sibylla comes to call Liberace, will be in attendance. Sibylla has an awkward encounter with him. He approaches her and, clearly meaning to flirt, asks, "Are you as bored and frustrated as you look?" Sibylla evades the question but comes to realize that she may be taking Liberace's query too literally. "Some people," she complains, "would see that until you have determined how bored and frustrated you look you have no way of knowing whether your sentiments match your appearance" (64).

Unfortunately, *other* people, people such as Liberace, fail to understand the illogic of their own words. Sibylla can't shake the man. He persists in coming on to her and follows her when she leaves, offering her a ride home. But he can't find where he parked his car, and so they end up walking to his apartment. All the while, Liberace talks "on and on and on" (69). At his apartment, they drink more, and he talks "more and more and more and asked more and more if he was boring me, and as a result it seemed less and less possible to leave, because if he wasn't boring me why would I want to leave?" (69). She finally decides that kissing him might be the easiest way to shut him up, and from there they proceed to sleep together.

We would not be wrong to find Sibylla's response to Liberace not only uncompromising but also comically obtuse. The travel writer's style of illogic is hardly unusual or surprising. It's the very fuel of small talk and flirtation, and the man's commercial success is nothing if not evidence that his brand of sociable illogic can elsewhere find a welcoming audience.

At moments like this, Sibylla's unwavering commitment to a narrowly conceived rationality becomes the object of the novel's satire.

By light of this satire, Sibylla and Liberace each evince complementary aesthetic and moral failings, though one would be hard pressed to find any virtues in Liberace. Ludo, in this scenario, would promise allegorically to close the distance between two failure modes, exemplified by the specialized scholarly press and the conglomerate bestseller factory. Sibylla would embody the cloistered, perhaps naïve, sensibility of the small academic press, Liberace the worldly conglomerate that acquires it. Liberace likewise absorbs Sibylla, threatening her autonomy, subordinating her fussy rationality under his wooly, voluble illogic. Another allegorical mapping might also fit: We can see Sibylla as standing in the position of the author, navigating the field of creation, and Liberace as a kind of editor, operating in the conglomerated field of production, interpreting her words in whatever way best serves his interests. On this reading, Ludo would be the product of their uneasy collaboration: someone whose existence depends on the field of production but whose ultimate allegiances are with the author.

We might find each of these specific readings more or less plausible, but we don't need to read the allegory at such a high level of resolution to understand its shape. On either reading, the relationship between Sibylla and Liberace is roughly the same. A scene of literary interpretation (really, misinterpretation) maps unequal access to power, capital, and prestige. It's not merely that Liberace doesn't recognize the illogic of asking if you're as bored and frustrated as you look—it's that he doesn't *need* to recognize it. The possibility that Sibylla's perspective might be worth taking seriously isn't even a consideration. Sibylla, meanwhile, is expected to conform to the travel writer's popular illogic. Moreover, gender categories structure the difference in power between them. Yet in this unequal exchange, as DeWitt represents it, the person in the subordinate position has access to a kernel of truth and rationality the person in the superordinate position has either thoughtlessly discarded or is structurally unable to see. DeWitt's allegory thus dramatizes one of the core arguments of feminist standpoint epistemology—that structural disadvantage confers epistemic advantages. This would be a scene of pure exploitation, another story of bad and powerful people triumphing over good and weak people, except for the fact that a child emerges from this union. If Sibylla and Liberace's sexual union might be read as reproducing the dynamics of an unwelcome corporate merger, we might ask whether that union will produce synergy.

Sibylla would have us believe that Ludo's task is simple: to reject his father's patrimony. To grow up successfully, he'll need to understand why it was rational of her not to introduce him to his father. Yet Liberace was a necessary condition for Ludo's creation. The questions of parental inheritance that dominate the novel—Ludo's quest for a father—look somewhat different if read as corporate allegory. The question isn't which values Ludo will adopt but which prose style he will embody. Might art emerge from such a merger? The allegory's answer is almost too perfect. Ludo rejects the illogic and thoughtlessness of his father, but he's also unable to accept the strict-but-sclerotic rationality his mother proffers. The boy is a sort of aesthetic miracle, a symbolic solution to an intractable problem. Though Ludo finally decides not to reveal his identity to his father and rejects the man, he also goes beyond his mother's commitments. Indeed, he not only surpasses his mother but *saves* her.

Ludo's quest to find an aesthetic form of life, which is also a moral form of life, recapitulates DeWitt's quest to find a workable form for her book. *The Last Samurai* is neither, as Jonathan Burnham thought, the story of a mother's love for her son nor, as DeWitt claimed, about what a mother must sacrifice for her son; it is a fantasy that your child (here a figure for your own novel) might outlive you, might achieve its own autonomy, might gain widespread popularity without compromising rigor, and might even, in some sense, save you, despite its misbegotten corporate parentage.

IV

The Last Samurai invests all its hopes in Ludo. It does so, according to the reading I have been developing, at several linked allegorical levels. First, within the world of the book, the novel sets up the reader to hope

that Ludo will, ultimately, save Sibylla. In realizing his potential, that
is, the son will develop the ingenuity and resources to save the mother.
Early in the novel, Sibylla observes of Ludo that "not every genius is a
prodigy & not every prodigy is a genius" (27). *The Last Samurai* might be
seen as a sequence of stories about prodigies who, for one reason or
another, fail to become geniuses. But if Ludo's quest shows him to be
not only a prodigy but also a genius, then his status retroactively redeems
Sibylla; she too might be a genius, whose genius might be to have out-
flanked a world that was threatening to destroy her in the same way that
it destroyed her father. This retroactive redemption applies, too, to the
second level of the allegory. *The Last Samurai* begins in a digressive and
fragmented style, which dramatizes Sibylla's disordered mind. But it
resolves into Ludo's neat sequence of lucid fable-like narratives.

That is, Ludo represents the formal culmination of the novel's style,
a final reordering of Sibylla's disorder. DeWitt did write Ludo's chapters before she wrote Sibylla's, but the novel only succeeds, only achieves
its aesthetic aims, if Ludo's part succeeds. And Ludo's quest is more than
a quest for a father; it's also a quest for a style of art, which is also a moral
style, that might navigate between the two poles represented by Sibylla
and Liberace, between uncompromising purity and gregarious vapidity,
between the scholarly and the worldly. Can these positions, which seem
mutually contradictory, be synthesized? In what follows, I argue that
each candidate father Ludo encounters embodies a different answer to
this question. Each fails for a different reason, until Ludo abandons his
quest—and, in abandoning his quest, discovers its true and secret nature.

Each candidate father fails Ludo's test for a different reason. But the
succession of fathers takes us, and Ludo, on a journey from Liberace's
naïve sincerity through various forms of masculine cynicism to a new
sincerity.[20] The first candidate father, Hugh Carey (HC), represents an
opportunity for Ludo to get the kind of education his biological father
thought inappropriate for his other children. As we have already discussed, HC is a scholar and an adventurer, who—"weary of philology,"
wanting to "go where all utterances died with breath"—searches for "a
strange silent tribe in the desert of Kyzylkum" (301). He eventually finds
the tribe, but at a terrible cost; HC impregnates a woman in the tribe,

but because he was fathered by a foreigner the son is sold into slavery. Ludo reflects, "He had not killed to learn those moodless verbs and uninflected nouns, but he had brought a slave into existence for their sake" (326). He also fails as a father because he fails to recognize Ludo's ruse.

The next candidate, George Sorabji, a Nobel Prize–winning physicist and "Robert Donat lookalike," fails on similar grounds (335). He's famous, among other reasons, for having helped a boy named Iki-go-e (or Pete) from an Amazonian tribe learn advanced mathematics. His story also emphasizes that the pursuit of pure science requires a cynical commitment to wheeling and dealing for funding and institutional support. Sorabji believes Ludo's lie, thinking he must be his son by a former Australian lover, and offers to help the boy get into school. But when Ludo tells him the truth, the physicist attacks him, before regaining his composure. Like HC, Sorabji marries credulity with cynicism.

The next candidate is more promising. Watkins, an experimental painter, is less credulous, but he is no less cynical in pursuit of his art. He's famous for engaging in a series of artistic experiments in the representation of color. Among these is a set of gimmicky paintings. For one, he bathes himself in lamb's blood and smears a canvas with that blood. The painting, *Let Brown = Red*, sells for £150,000. It is suggested that, though Watkins is serious about his art, he's not above minting money by pandering to the market. At the same time, he is, we are told, "too clever to be obvious" (384). He follows *Let Brown = Red* by creating another series called *Let Blue = Blue*, in which he fills a bathtub with blue paint and creates similar canvases. The artist immediately sees through Ludo's ruse and has no interest in adopting Ludo or mentoring him. But he does give Ludo a parting gift: a silk handkerchief with two thumb prints, one his (in ink), the other Ludo's (made with Ludo's blood). The title is *Washed white in the Blood of the Lamb*, an allusion to the hymn, which Ludo has previously sung for the artist. *Washed white in the Blood of the Lamb* is, on the one hand, a supremely cynical work, meant as a near-cash-equivalent gift to Ludo. On the other, it will play a key role in the novel's allegory of art production under capitalism, and it of course also aligns Ludo's blood with the blood of Christ. Watkins has mastered the art of moving between different registers of value. He's devised a practice that allows him to turn specific aesthetic gestures (quite literally) into capital. But he has, arguably, also compromised his art.

The next two fathers are less cynical but still fail Ludo's test. Mustafa Szegeti, the gambler and quasi-diplomat, immediately sees through Ludo's ruse and apprehends the reasoning behind the boy's deception. "You could say it [that I was your father] to me because it wasn't true? he [tells Ludo]. I see!" (413). But what he cannot do is help Ludo make sense of Sibylla's history of suicidal ideation. The boy wants the gambler to make a pronouncement on whether Sibylla would be better off alive or dead, but the man evades the question and essentially sends Ludo away. The next candidate, the journalist Red Devlin, also sees through Ludo's ruse but seems willing to accept the boy as his son. The only problem is that he's about to commit suicide when Ludo encounters him. Ludo spends time with Red Devlin, gets a VHS tape for him from Blockbuster Video, and eats fish and chips with him. Ludo hopes to find some way to convince the journalist not to commit suicide, but nothing works. Devlin is, Ludo concludes after the man finally kills himself, the father he wishes he had. He doesn't think he can do better. Devlin is a model of manly integrity and consistency. Yet Devlin cannot give Ludo the resources he will need to help Sibylla, and his devotion to his family doesn't prevent him from succumbing to his suicidal ideation. Here, Ludo's quest seems to come to an end, but in fact his true purpose is revealed. When Mustafa Szegeti and Red Devlin both, for a moment, seem to accept Ludo as a possible surrogate son, Ludo discovers that what he wants from these two models of manly virtue is help for his mother. That is, their example shows Ludo that he actually doesn't want to find a father after all; rather, he wants to find a way to rescue his mother. But they can't give Ludo what he really needs.

The solution to this new problem comes in the form of another masculine role model: the avant-garde pianist Kenzo Yamamoto. We are introduced to Yamamoto early in the novel. He seems to replicate Sibylla's aesthetic commitments. He's interested in thinking of the piano as a percussion instrument since, in his view, "any sound that the instrument could make was obviously a sound it could make" (150). Artists are, he thinks, "afraid of the surface [of music] . . . afraid it will sound like what it is" (151). His theory of music is that "music was not about sound but about perception of sound which means in a sense that to perceive what it is you need also some sense of what it could be but is not which includes other types of sounds and also silence" (157). And: "what you saw was that it was perceiving these fragments as fragments that made it possible to have a real conception of what wholeness might be in a work" (158).

In pursuit of these commitments, Yamamoto performs a series of experimental concerts in which he plays variations and fragments of classical compositions. At one concert, which Sibylla and Ludo attend, he plays a seemingly interminable set of variations through the night. Most of the audience leaves, but Sibylla has a powerful aesthetic experience. She concludes, clearly relating her experience of Yamamoto's art to her life's myriad disappointments:

> You could have a thing 500 ways without giving up one he [Yamamoto] said No, there is only one chance at life once gone it is gone for good you must seize the moment before it goes, tears were streaming down my face as I heard these three pieces each with just one chance of being heard if there was a mistake then the piece was played just once with a mistake if there was some other way to play the piece you heard what you heard and it was time to go home.
>
> (163)

Though he's introduced before HC, Yamamoto's first performance answers HC's desire to overcome scholarship and philology. If HC wants to find a society in which "all utterances died with breath," Yamamoto constructs an art form that is self-immolating, used up in its moment of enunciation. Its artistic power is tied up with its ephemerality. But as a model of art it seems, at first at least, utterly unsustainable and constitutively uncommodifiable. After two concerts performed in this uncompromising style, it seems unlikely that Yamamoto will have an opportunity to play again in a major venue. In its rigor, Yamamoto's pure art destroys itself.

When Ludo meets Yamamoto, at the end of the novel, the man is practicing piano alone. Ludo hears variations of Charles-Valentin Alkan's *Le festin d'Ésope* playing on Marylebone Road. The final étude of his *12 Études dans tous les tons mineurs, Op. 39* is a work of twenty-five variations on a theme, which require exceptional skill to play. The title refers to the story of Aesop's feast. In the legend, Aesop's master Xanthus asks him to prepare a fine meal for his guests. Aesop serves a meal consisting entirely of tongues, averring that all philosophy and education are made possible because of tongues. Aesop's master, annoyed, commands him next to serve a meal of what is "the most worthless, the most inferior thing there is," and Aesop again serves a meal of tongues, suggesting that the tongue contains all that is bad because it is the cause of "enmity, plots, battles, rivalry, strife, wars."[21]

It is, I'd suggest, no accident that Ludo's recognition of this étude leads him to the successful resolution of his revised quest. First, the fable of "The Tongues" might be viewed as a paradigmatic encyclopedic narrative, in which a single image—the tongue—comes to stand in for all art and learning and all human misery. The tongue is a figure for the totality of human knowledge. Yet it's also clear that the fable positions the slave as better equipped to articulate this totality than the master. Aesop—traditionally represented as ugly, deformed, dark skinned, hunchbacked—outwits his master, to the delight and approval of the dinner guests. This image of encyclopedic virtuosity from below offers an allegorical referent for Alkan, whose étude represents the culmination of *12 Études dans tous les tons mineurs, Op. 39*.

Alkan is himself also a figure for the exacting genius who withdraws from public life in part because he is, as Ludo tells Yamamoto, "passed over for the directorship of the Conservatoire through sordid political machinations in favour of a mediocrity and so condemned to a life of bitter obscurity" (474). Yet another bitter genius!

Informed by the confidence of Red Devlin, Ludo cons his way past the woman who greets him at Yamamoto's door and meets the man himself. Yamamoto tells him he no longer gives concerts because he keeps "giving the wrong size of concert" (477). Ludo asks him why he doesn't make a CD, and Yamamoto replies by saying, "No one would buy the kind of thing I'd like to put on a CD and I can't afford to make a CD that no one will buy" (477). He wants to make a CD that consists of "variations on variations on variations." Only "5 people would buy" it. Ludo, of course, can now afford "to make a CD that no one will buy." He will sell Watkins's cynical market-oriented artwork and redeem it for a work of pure art microtargeted at Sibylla. Ludo's literal blood, consecrated by the artist, now bearer of market value, will redeem his mother.

At this moment, Ludo becomes the fulfilled fantasy of a good middleman. He navigates a cynical art market and sees how to leverage his advantages, intelligence, and financial resources to commission a work that has the potential to delight and maybe save his mother. This opportunity for Sibylla's redemption comes at the end of a long chain of improbable encounters. Ludo is finally able to convince Yamamoto to make the CD by offering to teach him to play Thelonious Monk's "Straight, No Chaser," which he has learned by listening to "the tape & trying to copy it about 500 times" (33). Of course, "Straight, No Chaser" offers another variation of Yamamoto's approach to making art. The composition "involves basically only one idea played again and again, each time in a different part of the measure and with a different ending." These variations "reflect a craftsmanship that can produce depth in simplicity."[22]

Yamamoto agrees to this exchange with one word:

Done.

(482)

This is, of course, also the last word of the novel. Yamamoto's "Done" signals the fulfillment not only of Ludo's quest but also of the novel's mission. What more is there to say? DeWitt announces what we already suspect: that Ludo's success and the success of the novel are inseparable. In other words, *The Last Samurai* itself comes retroactively to be positioned as a work of art that hopes it might become its own canny middleman. Might the novel have the resources to pull off Ludo's trick: to navigate a minefield of commerce, broken contemporary sociological structures, and save its author? I would underscore, again, the overdetermination of the different fields Clayton Childress analyzes. Ludo's aesthetic education (his mastery of the field of creation) is also an education in self-promotion and marketing (the field of production), as well as an education that considers its audience (the field of reception).

It's not that Ludo finds a safe harbor of aesthetic autonomy away from the tumultuous seas of the open market. Rather, Ludo's canny ability to navigate the market becomes the very precondition for the aesthetic autonomy Sibylla values. Sibylla's redemption has a literal and specific cash value. What artists need isn't autonomy. It's money.

V

At one point in *The Last Samurai*, Ludo questions the consistency of his mother's reverence for *Seven Samurai*. He suggests that by his mother's standards, "Seven Samurai can't be any good because it's in black and white and Japanese" (230). Sibylla scoffs at the charge. "There is an obvious difference," she explains, "between someone who works within the technical limitations of his time which are beyond his control and someone who accepts without thinking limitations which are entirely within his own power to set aside" (230–31). The supposed obviousness of what is and isn't "entirely within [one's] power to set aside" is a central concern of *The Last Samurai*, one that speaks to the challenge DeWitt faced when seeking a publisher. Is a sociological structure a limitation beyond the ability of the artist to control? Can the author simply "set aside" norms of publishing, storytelling, and propriety she finds uncongenial? What can Sibylla—or Ludo, or DeWitt—ignore or set aside? What kind of "power" is required to set aside or to accept limitations? And what is the relation between "thinking" and "power"?

The Last Samurai offers various answers to these questions. In part, it answers these questions through its representation of successful or achieved artworks. There is, of course, Kurosawa's *Seven Samurai*, the repeated viewings of which sustain Sibylla and inspire Ludo. Yet how one should interpret *Seven Samurai*'s achievement isn't clear. Ludo doesn't simply replicate his mother's interpretation, and as DeWitt notes, Sibylla does not "inculcate her own understanding of the film" upon the boy.[23] Yamamoto represents another model of the successful artist. The variations upon variations Yamamoto performs—a practice linked to Aesop, Charles-Valentin Alkan, and Thelonious Monk—seem to exemplify a kind of art Sibylla would endorse. Yet Yamamoto is, in the end, unable to bring his art to market without Ludo's market-redeemed blood. And the strategy of independently producing a CD is, itself, conditioned by the technical possibilities afforded by relatively cheap digital reproduction. In the 1990s, when DeWitt was seeking her own artistic fortunes, such avenues of self-publication were not as easily available, though the storage format of the CD might be read as a figure for a world in which artists have the technical means to sidestep official distribution and publication channels.[24]

What Yamamoto's inability to sustainably make art suggests is that there's a gap between Sibylla's and DeWitt's position on the form achieved art might take. It would be a mistake to equate author and character without further elaboration. At the very least, we must recognize that DeWitt's artistic practice and Sibylla's intellectual commitments often part ways. For DeWitt, the artist should not simply ignore inconvenient sociological structures but seek to transform them. Doing so doesn't require that the artist withdraw from the marketplace but actively shapes the conditions of publication. Such intervention isn't only part of the story of the making of *The Last Samurai* but also figured within the novel. Ludo's sections were, as I've mentioned, the first DeWitt wrote, but in the revised and completed version of the book, his fable-like style, the variations upon variations of his quest the novel runs through, become the *formal solution* to Sibylla's tortured quest to find a workable style. Sibylla is trapped in a cyclical narrative. Ludo rushes forward, albeit through a dialectical sequence of variations of the same scene. The mother's perfectionism and exactitude give way to a more labile and welcoming sensibility in the child. In this relative openness, we would not be wrong to notice a trace of Liberace.

How can a boy save his impoverished, suicidal mother? How might a novel save its author, especially in a world dominated by conglomerate publishing? If the job of the novel is to emerge from contemporary publishing without compromising itself, what does an achieved work of art look like in the present? These questions are not allegorical synonyms, but *The Last Samurai* aligns them and stages a set of answers, ultimately giving Ludo the resources he'll need to solve the riddle. Such, anyway, is the novel's fantasy of the power of art (and its own power). But that literary fantasy, unfortunately for DeWitt, had to confront the actual publishing world. Imaginary solutions to real contradictions are, alas, still only imaginary. Which is to say, the story of making of *The Last Samurai* is far from done.

4

FUCK *THE CHICAGO MANUAL OF STYLE*

I

Jonathan Burnham stopped the taxi; he had to go home. The car pulled over, and he jumped out, leaving Helen DeWitt behind. DeWitt had been talking to him about problems with the production process of her novel, but her editor had, she explained to me, a "pathological aversion" to discussing the topic.[1] Even twenty years later, talking to me in Leisure World, her mother's retirement community in Silver Spring, Maryland, DeWitt's exasperation was evident. It made no sense! Copyediting is a normal part of publishing, the most ordinary thing. And DeWitt had flown from Chesterfield in England to New York specifically to get her book ready for press in a hurry. Talk Miramax had paid for her transatlantic trip; Burnham wined and dined her. But when DeWitt tried to explain the problems she was having with her copyeditor, he would change the subject. He wouldn't answer her questions. At one point, he suggested they see a ballet together. During the intermission, he said he wanted to leave the show. In the taxi, she tried again to get clarity on the copyedits, at which point Burnham quit the scene.[2]

"How emotionally charged can [copyediting] possibly be?" DeWitt asked me.[3]

It was the winter of 1999. After its success at the Frankfurt Book Fair, *The Last Samurai* was on the fast track. It would be published in under a year. When DeWitt signed her contract with Talk Miramax, she was represented not by an agent but by the entertainment lawyer Larry Shire. The contract gave her right of final approval on the manuscript but also required her personally to clear permissions for quotes, which turned into a slog. The Kurosawa estate allowed her to use quotes from *Seven Samurai* but rejected her title. "The Seventh Samurai" became *The Last Samurai.*

As a writer, DeWitt needed large uninterrupted blocks of time to work. Two years after she had shelved the project, *The Last Samurai* was far removed from her artistic concerns. But she felt a duty to give her troubled book a chance, so she put other projects on hold. Though he originally considered requesting major revisions to the novel, Burnham ultimately did not request serious changes. Still, DeWitt had never completed a final version of the manuscript, so she very quickly made long-deferred editorial decisions and submitted the book. When the copyedits came back, DeWitt discovered her manuscript had been changed in unsettling ways.

The copyeditor had incorporated a systematic distinction between *that* and *which*, in line with the view that *that* is obligatory in restrictive clauses. DeWitt had not heard of this distinction before—and her prose didn't obey it. The copyeditor also introduced periods into acronyms and initialisms that reflected her understanding of American usage. When DeWitt asked her how she decided where to include periods, DeWitt's copyeditor told her that she did what "felt right."[4] DeWitt had, for her part, tried rigorously to distinguish between American and British usage, using different patterns of period usage in different sections of the novel.[5] Words written in all caps were changed to italics or small caps, a change Dewitt regarded as "absurd."

This was all bad enough, but the most significant changes the copyeditor introduced concerned numbers. The *Chicago Manual of Style* suggests that the numbers one hundred and below should be spelled out. But DeWitt liked the convention the *Guardian* followed, in which numerals are used for all numbers above ten. This usage, DeWitt said, reminded her of a favorite novel of hers, Russell Hoban's *Riddley Walker,* in which numbers are always written with numerals. DeWitt wanted to use numerals instead of spelled-out numbers to mirror how her characters think in mathematical terms and to dramatize Ludo's obsession with numbers and advanced mathematics.

DeWitt prepared to defend her usage. She consulted authoritative sources such as *Fowler's Dictionary of Modern English Usage*, which supported the view that the *that-which* distinction isn't a hard-and-fast rule. Indeed, British English tends to use the terms interchangeably more often than American English. DeWitt also cited her own academic study of propriety, noting that poetic and literary style, by definition, departs from norms of ordinary usage. Departing from ordinary usage is what makes literary language *literary* in the first place! Moreover, standards of correctness face special difficulty when confronted with literary departures from the norm. Breaking established rules has long been one characteristic of great oratory. "These rules are not handed down by God," DeWitt told me. If you unthinkingly rely on *The Chicago Manual of Style* to determine usage, you foreclose the possibility that punctuation and typography might be used for expressive purposes.

DeWitt responded to the changes her copyeditor introduced into her book, justifying her preferred usage at length. She began writing what she described as, in effect, a book-length commentary on punctuation and usage for her novel. But she was working on a tight schedule, and her manuscript was more than five hundred pages, so she eventually stopped explaining her reversals and simply started stetting the copyeditor's alterations. DeWitt had negotiated final approval of the manuscript, but Kristin Powers, the production assistant at Talk Miramax, preferred the copyeditor's version of the text. Burnham too was inclined to agree with Powers, worrying that DeWitt's version risked looking "careless" and like a "mistake."[6] DeWitt brought copies of *All the Pretty Horses* and *The Autobiography of Alice B. Toklas* to the Talk Miramax office to show canonical examples of nonstandard orthography and punctuation, but Burnham was not persuaded.

Talk Miramax undoubtedly had its own institutional concerns. Any book Talk published would reflect not only on its author but also on the fledgling publisher that spent a great deal of money to acquire it. The whole industry was scrutinizing them. With an office of only four people, Burnham's position felt especially precarious. To deviate from industry norms, to produce books that might, on casual visual inspection, seem sloppy or careless, was a risk Burnham likely wanted to avoid. And *The Last Samurai* was Talk Miramax's first major literary acquisition. Whatever his justification, Burnham's resistance was not well received. After one especially contentious meeting, DeWitt stormed out of the office and considered withdrawing her novel and publishing it on her own. She drafted a long and detailed letter explaining her position, but in the end did not need to send it. Burnham had, DeWitt learned, spoken to his boyfriend, Joe Dolce, who'd apparently said, in response to Burnham's concerns, "Fuck *The Chicago Manual of Style!*"[7]

This—in DeWitt's telling, at least—settled the matter. Burnham was now persuaded to support her, to let her publish *The Last Samurai* in her preferred typographic form. Victory in hand, DeWitt returned to the United Kingdom. But in January 2000, she received galley proofs of the novel and discovered that the copyeditor's changes remained unreversed. Almost none of her stetting had been implemented. DeWitt demanded to see the original manuscript to confirm her suspicion and discovered many—though not all—of her reversals had been erased with Wite-Out. Changes where she had written a note explaining her reversals remained; many of the rest were gone. DeWitt spoke again with Burnham on the phone and made a second, rapid round of edits to the galley proof. After an arduous, last-minute round of editing, DeWitt's preferences finally did appear in the published version of the novel. But the production process was crushing.

"If they had sent a team to my house," she explained, "and just taken a truncheon and smashed my computer and taken my books and stripped the place bare, people would see that as outrageous. But if they just kill the mind that wrote the book, they don't see that as bad."[8]

II

DeWitt's struggle with her copyeditor has received considerable journalistic attention. It's an interesting story and makes for a good hook. There's a narrative pleasure to be had in figuring literary history as the conflict between strong-willed personalities who have cinematic fights. But is there more to say about the conflict? Why did these typographic choices matter so much to DeWitt? Why would reversing them amount to killing "the mind that wrote the book"? What difference do usage and punctuation make for understanding and interpreting *The Last Samurai?* And what or whom are you fucking when you fuck *The Chicago Manual of Style?* In this chapter, I offer preliminary answers to these questions, suggesting that DeWitt's combat with her copyeditor has interpretive consequences. Copyediting—a process almost undiscussed by scholars of contemporary literature—matters.[9]

I focus especially on the novel's representation of numbers.

As mentioned earlier, DeWitt wanted to connect a style of representing numbers to a style of thought. Her characters think mathematically and therefore reflexively write numbers using numerals. From the opening pages of the novel, Sibylla discusses her family history in statistical and probabilistic terms. Born to a Methodist minister, Sibylla's father is an "ardent atheist" (3). Sibylla tells us that "he skipped grades the way other boys skip class, he lectured my grandfather's flock on carbon 14 and the origin of species, and he won a full scholarship to Harvard at the age of 15" (3).

This sentence is deceptively straightforward. The verb tenses "skipped," "lectured," and "won" are in the simple past but paint a portrait of the habitual past. Sibylla's father not only skips grades but is *the sort of person* who skips grades. It's not clear whether he actually lectures his father's flock or is just a person who does *that sort of thing*. The choice of "carbon 14" seems meant not only to emphasize the father's scientific cast of mind but also to highlight his age, written as "15." This opening paragraph immediately and subtly alerts us that we're in the presence of a mind (Sibylla's) that thinks in statistical and probabilistic terms. Sibylla is here trying to impose order upon, and to make sense of her relation to, her own and her family's troubled history. Sibylla's father's story also anticipates the parable-like style of Ludo's sections, suggesting the mathematical precision Sibylla aspires to embody is linked to the simplified yet highly architected form of the folktale. When Sibylla's grandfather tells her father that he shouldn't accept the scholarship he has received to Harvard and that he should instead "give the other side [the side of organized religion] a chance," the father applies to three seminaries—the first two of which, in folktale-like fashion, reject him. The third accepts him.

Sibylla's father comes to bitterly regret his decision not to attend Harvard; his father, he concludes, has ruined his life, consigning him to a tedious, meaningless existence. But he does not lose all hope, or he at least tries to convince himself that some chance for a better life remains available to him. Sometimes, Sibylla tells us, her father would give money to a stranger:

> He'd say, Here's fifty bucks, if you happen to go to Monte Carlo do me a favor, go to the roulette table and put this on number 17 and keep it there for 17 spins of the wheel, the man would say he wasn't planning to go to Monte Carlo and my father would say But if you do and he'd give him his card. Because what were the odds that the man would change his plans and go to Monte Carlo, what were the odds that 17 would come up 17 times in a row, what were the odds that if it did the man would send the money on to my father? Whatever they were it was not absolutely impossible but only highly unlikely, and it was not absolutely certain that my grandfather had destroyed him because there was a 1 in 500 trillion trillion trillion chance that he had not.
>
> (8–9)

Sibylla's father clearly doesn't expect to see any returns from this occasional gamble. The money he gives away is, instead, meant to highlight his bitterness and the (in-effect) absolute certainty that his life has been destroyed. Yet in Sibylla's telling, the destruction of her father's life becomes the condition of possibility for her own existence. It's because her father goes to seminary instead of Harvard that he meets her uncle Buddy, and through Buddy Linda, Buddy's youngest sister—Sibylla's mother. In fact, the claim that there's a "1 in 500 trillion trillion trillion chance" that the father's life has not been destroyed immediately precedes the introduction of Linda. The implication seems to be that his meeting Linda is kind of like winning the lottery, a low-probability high-value turn of fortune.

Of course, the story of how Sibylla's parents met is told retrospectively, by Sibylla. Sibylla's father might tell his own story differently. For

Sibylla, her father's story frames her own, and his misery and thwarted potential anticipate her own crisis. The question of whether her parents' meeting redeems her father's bad choices directly speaks to whether her own life has been similarly "destroyed." We might presume that Sibylla has an interest in her own existence, but her history of suicidal ideation complicates that presumption. Sibylla is, as we have noted, committed to adhering to what she describes as the most stringent standard of rationality. She sees few honest reasons to hope that her misery will abate but nonetheless struggles to find some rational basis to justify her continued existence. It's therefore significant that Sibylla describes Ludo's conception in a way that uses a statistical frame that resembles the one she has already put around her family's life.

She writes: "There are 60 million people in Britain. There are 200 million in America. (Can that be right?) How many millions of English-speakers other nations might add to the total I cannot even guess. I would be willing to bet, though, that in all those hundreds of millions not more than 50, at the outside, have read A. Roemer, *Aristarchs Athetesen in der Homerkritik* (Leipzig, 1912), a work untranslated from its native German and destined to remain so till the end of time" (17). Sibylla constructs the widest possible demographic context for her story. Setting herself amid the planet's whole English-speaking population, she picks herself out not as an individual but as a type, one of fifty. Later, we come to understand the significance of this framing.

"I was about to say earlier," Sibylla explains, "that if I had not read Roemer on the 30th of April 1985 the world would be short a genius; I said that the world without the Infant Terrible would be like the world without Newton & Mozart & Einstein!" (27). As in the story of her father, the vector of Sibylla's seeming destruction (Roemer) might, in fact, turn out to be the means of her, and by extension her family's, salvation. Her reading Roemer might give the world a new "Newton & Mozart & Einstein!" Her father's lifetime of misery might, itself, cash out in the birth of a genius. What are the chances not only that Sibylla's encounter with the "insanity" of Roemer might be a condition of possibility for the birth of a genius? Perhaps "a 1 in 500 trillion trillion trillion chance." We can see, with greater clarity, the importance of DeWitt's representation of numbers, the layer of meaning that would be lost if the copyeditor had prevailed.

DeWitt uses numerals not only to emphasize Sibylla's stochastic cast of mind but also to dramatize the stakes of her emotional and intellectual struggle. Sibylla uses a mathematized narrative form (the fable) to make sense of her father's failure. She describes her own failures and her hopes for a better future in probabilistic terms, using such terms to ask existential questions about the meaning and purpose of her life. Indeed, in her quest to live a rational life, Sibylla more generally applies a utilitarian mode of thought to assess arguments about the rationality of suicide, again employing mathematized forms of representation. In one scene, riding the Circle Line, Sibylla has an argument with a stranger, discussing the rationality of suicide under certain conditions:

> Sibylla said let's take the example of two men about to be burned at the stake, A dies at time t of heart failure while B burns to death at time t + n, I think we can all agree that B's life would be better if it were n minutes shorter. The lady said she thought it was rather different and Sibylla said she thought it was exactly the same and the lady said there was no need to shout. Sibylla said she wasn't shouting she just thought it was barbaric to force people to die at time t + n and she said barbaric so loud that everyone in the train looked around!
>
> (112)

Sibylla's argument for suicide takes an algebraic narrative form, in which specific individuals are replaced, in the manner of many philosophical thought experiments, with variables (A, B) and where time is similarly reduced to a sequence of variables (t, t + n). This reduction, in this context, is meant to compel Sibylla's interlocutor to cede the rationality of suicide under certain circumstances. Of course, the fact that Sibylla ends the conversation by shouting at the other woman suggests that Sibylla is, herself, not always the bastion of rationality she aspires to be.

DeWitt's representation of Sibylla's reasoning about suicide is in dialogue with the philosophy of Jonathan Glover. In *Causing Death and Saving Lives*, Glover undertakes a broadly utilitarian analysis of the ethics of killing, while offering amendments to a strictly utilitarian account of the wrongness of killing that incorporates an understanding of the value of personal autonomy. In his discussion of suicide, Glover offers two principles for assessing whether preventing a suicide can be justified. Preventing suicide might be justified "to save a worth-while life," yet one also should "respect a person's autonomy," understanding that a person has a special right to make decisions that affect them and their future.[10]

Glover's analysis links the rationality of suicide to prospective vision, a probabilistic calculation of "how likely or unlikely is any improvement in [a suicidal person's] state." Someone contemplating suicide assesses the likelihood that their situation will improve. Glover doesn't disregard the possibility that one might decide suicide is the rational choice, but he suggests that we are often "bad at predicting our own futures." The person persuaded by suicidal lines of reasoning should, therefore, consider alternative living arrangements before following through with self-destruction—"leaving his family, changing his job, emigrating, or seeking psychiatric help."[11] DeWitt invokes and dramatizes the limits of Glover's utilitarianism in the face of actual suicidal ideation. When trying to persuade Red Devlin not to kill himself, Ludo cites *Causing Death and Saving Lives*, telling the journalist that Glover "says before committing suicide you should change your job, leave your wife, leave the country" (447). The appeal, of course, doesn't persuade Devlin.

Ludo's failure would seem to support the conclusion that the critics Caroline Marie and Christelle Reggiani reach about *The Last Samurai*. In a typology of how mathematics has been incorporated into contemporary literature, they suggest that DeWitt's novel ultimately *disavows* Sibylla's mathematicized way of seeing the world. "Becoming a samurai," they argue, "implies giving up the illusory quest of a perfectly mathematized reality in favour of the pragmatics of action, by nature unforeseeable and irreducible to axioms."[12] DeWitt would be suggesting that Ludo must learn what Sibylla fails to see: that strict adherence to standards of rationality and mathematized reconstructions of life can create its own forms of dysfunction.

On this view, *The Last Samurai* isn't ultimately endorsing the idea that we should see the world the way that Sibylla does. Sibylla's reconstruction of her family's history seems often to be a ramshackle defense mechanism.

At best, this mathematized way of seeing gives her imperfect terms for describing what it feels like to live in a society that thwarts human flourishing, a society that threatens to destroy Ludo in the way that she and her parents have been destroyed. But it doesn't offer much in the way of a "pragmatics of action." Math won't tell you how to live. The novel would ultimately be dramatizing the way mathematized thought might become not only a cognitive life preserver but also an anchor, dragging one down into an abyss. Ludo's mathematical obsessions, which at first seem to replicate his mother's characteristic style of thought, must give way to a more worldly way of being. One representational object of the novel's typographic choices would thus be nothing other than the attraction and the tragedy of mathematized thought. To change numerals into spelled-out numbers would erase, or mute, this dimension of the novel.

III

In the previous section, I've developed an interpretation of DeWitt's typographic choices, focusing especially on how the author's representation of numerals foregrounds a range of issues related to what I've called mathematized thought. What happens if you emplot the arc of a single life, or the life of a family, in probabilistic and statistical terms? How do we reckon the value of a life when we describe it not in its empirical specificity but as variables, according to a utilitarian calculus? These interpretations take us far in understanding why the novel's typographic playfulness matters, but it does risk focusing too much on the psychological particularities of DeWitt's characters. For Ludo's story, as we've seen, isn't only his own. It also stands in for DeWitt's vision of successful art. The stakes of the copyediting process of *The Last Samurai* likewise go beyond DeWitt's desire to find representational homologies for the situation of her characters. DeWitt may be representing—and critiquing—aspects of Sibylla's mathematized thought, but DeWitt is herself invested in thinking about how mathematics, probability, statistics, and information design might change the novel. This investment is connected to DeWitt's larger critique of the norms, standards, and institutional constraints that hem in artistic possibility. From DeWitt's perspective, her copyeditor was reproducing norms of propriety that allowed for only a narrow range of artistic expression.

Against such restrictions, DeWitt uses a language of mathematics to speak about the universe of unexplored possibilities available to the ambitious writer. Mathematical thought becomes a metaphor for her for an awareness of and multiplication of literary forms and the potential to make or discover new forms. DeWitt is, in short, a sort of formalist, albeit one who differs in significant ways from Russian formalism, as I discussed in chapter 2. For DeWitt, form becomes a battleground upon which artists must secure new artistic and personal freedoms. And as Anna Kornbluh shows, a specifically mathematical conception of formalism underwrites many historical formalist practices. Kornbluh defines mathematical formalism as a radical redefinition "of the scope and methods of math, elevating abstractions and their internal consistency above phenomena and their experiential measure."[13] Such formalisms "provide structure for new possibles."

For those tutored by mathematical formalism, potential (as opposed to actual) form becomes newly salient as an object of artistic understanding. The formalist is interested in not only particular features of particular novels but also an abstracted vision of The Novel, which presides above merely existing novels. Literary history becomes, on this view, a procession of rising and declining forms—the rise of the novel, the decline of epic, and so on. And given the unavailability of any actual texts from the future, the formalist sees the future of literature as new combinations of form, "new possibles," as Kornbluh puts it. Such an understanding of form, I would emphasize, is held not only by critics but also by working artists. For the formalist writer, the creative act is partly a matter of devising new forms.

For her part, as we have seen, DeWitt repeatedly suggests that literary history is a history of the recombination of existing forms and the invention of new forms. DeWitt found her calling as a novelist, let's recall, because she became enchanted with "all [the] possibilities" her ex-husband David Levene had exposed her to. And let's also recall that Sibylla suggests that the destiny of the novel lies in the aesthetic interrogation (and integration) of elements of form authors have historically ignored—"the monosyllables and lack of grammatical inflection in Chinese," "lovely long Finnish words all double letters & long vowels in 14 cases," "lovely Hungarian all prefixes suffixes." The job of the serious artist is to activate dimensions of form that have remained invisible or latent to literary history.

This commitment—the commitment to activating new elements of form—is not only Sibylla's but to an extent also DeWitt's. Beyond *The Last Samurai*, DeWitt's fiction often associates mathematized thought with literary innovation. This association is evident in stories published in her collection *Some Trick*. For example, "My Heart Belongs to Bertie," which tells the story of an author of "robot tales," features multiple graphs created with R, a programming language for statistical computing DeWitt has long had an interest in.[14] DeWitt wrote the story partly to find a "way to make non-intuitive ways of thinking about probability visible on the page."[15] Pursuing this aim, she has investigated data visualization and design, often referring to the work of the political scientist Edward Tufte as an influence.

DeWitt's 2017 short story "Sexual Codes of the Europeans: A Preliminary Report," which was inspired by Italo Calvino's novel *Invisible Cities*, imagines a world in which "codes for communicating sexual preferences" are "like the bidding system of bridge."[16] The story presents itself, initially, as if it were a series of blog posts that give "the sexual codes for 5 provincial European cities" and then traces the stories of various travelers who go to these cities and deploy the codes.[17] Here and elsewhere, DeWitt is interested in creating literature at the limit of established form, pursuing experiments she thinks might "change the face of C21 fiction."[18]

DeWitt's writing practice is clearly partly inspired by Oulipo (Ouvroir de Littérature Potentielle), a group of mostly French mathematicians and writers who sought (and still seek) to explore untapped possibilities in literary art. Founded in 1960 by François Le Lionnais and Raymond Queneau, Oulipo has promoted the practice of reworking existing texts and established literary forms using new formulas and new constraints. Though part of a lineage of the avant-garde and 1960s conceptualism, members of Oulipo notably tend to invoke mathematics as part of the rationale for their experimental practice. Le Lionnais and Queneau were inspired by Nicolas Bourbaki, a group of French mathematicians who wrote under a collective pseudonym, which sought to focus on "pure mathematics"—writing collectively on set theory, abstract algebra, topology, and other topics. Though their preferred analogies with mathematics shouldn't necessarily be taken at face value, Oulipo was interested in exploring literary problems at a higher level of abstraction than their predecessors. A notion of the "constraint" was the primary unit of Oulipian innovation, although, as Gérard Genette suggests, Oulipian constraints are often specifically *transformational* in nature. That is, they tend to take an existing text and change it systematically, to produce new a text with new meanings.[19]

The group produced many classics. Raymond Queneau's *Exercices de style* (1947) retells the same story—the story of an altercation on a bus—in ninety-nine different styles. His *Cent mille milliards de poèmes* (1961) is a text-machine that allows readers to procedurally generate an enormous number of "new" sonnets. Georges Perec's *La disparition* (1969; trans. *A Void*) is a novel famously written without the letter *e*. His *La vie mode d'emploi* (1978, trans. as *Life: A User's Manual*) uses a variety of constraints to tell the story of a single apartment block in Paris. Anne Françoise Garréta's *Sphinx* (1986) rigorously avoids gender markers to describe its characters.

Italo Calvino is a frequent point of reference for DeWitt, including in her self-published collaborative novel *Your Name Here*, which invokes *If on a winter's night a traveler* (1979). Yet there's a significant difference between Oulipo's formalism and DeWitt's. Oulipo is usually taken to be programmatically *antiexpressive*, at odds with received notions of authorhood and creative genius, pursuing a mathematized impersonality that might advance literary art but not necessarily by promoting or centering the author.[20] As Joshua Clover observes, Oulipo joined a highly specific flourishing of theorizations on the "death of the author" in the late 1960s, posing its practice against expressivity, genius, and originality.[21] Oulipo's "Lipo: First Manifesto" reads: "That which certain writers have introduced with talent (even with genius) in their work, some only occasionally (the forging of new words), others with predilection (counterrhymes), others with insistence but in only one direction (Lettrism), the Ouvroir de Littérature Potentielle (Oulipo) intends to do systematically and scientifically, if need be through recourse to machines that process information."[22] Oulipo replaces the figure of the author with a text-making machine. For those working within this paradigm, literary forms work themselves out within a conceptual possibility space. The rise of this way of talking about textual production corresponds, in Clover's account, with the historical "dematerialization" of the art object—itself, he argues, a symptom of the end of the era of rapid growth at midcentury and the rise of deindustrialization.

DeWitt shares much with Oulipo's way of thinking about artistic creation. She's not committed to an ideology of "subjective expressivity"—the notion that the creative writer expresses some authentic kernel of self through their writing. It was, of course, some version of this notion that conceptual artists and poststructuralist critics sought to deconstruct. Yet DeWitt also sometimes describes the recombinational potential of the novel in specifically *expressive* or *personal* terms. In her account, the mind of the author has something special to offer to the process of art making. *The Last Samurai* complicates standard understandings of genius—the novel suggests that knowing who is and isn't a genius is more difficult than we might imagine under existing social conditions—but DeWitt doesn't abandon the idea of genius altogether.[23]

Here, I think, attending once again to DeWitt's education as a classicist squares the circle. When I asked her if she had any formal training as a creative writer, DeWitt told me she didn't. But she did describe Greek and Latin prose composition translation exercises she undertook at Oxford that might be thought of as a sort of literary training. Classics students at Oxford would be given a paragraph of a modern text—say *Alice in Wonderland*—to translate into Greek or Latin. They'd be required to translate the modern sensibility of the text back into a classical language—while still writing idiomatically. DeWitt found these exercises fiendishly difficult but also extremely enjoyable; they posed not only the usual problems of translation but required wit and style to complete successfully.

After completing this exercise, students were given a fair copy of the translation, that is, an example of the translation that succeeded especially well at the task, solving all the technical challenges of rendering modern prose into passable Latin or Greek. DeWitt remembers being delighted by the successful examples, which both solved thorny technical problems and managed to do so elegantly. What this scene of classical training suggests is that DeWitt in many ways sees herself more as a rhetorician than a creative writer in a conventional mode. Writing is a practice of solving challenges that allow one to go on to the next challenge. When asked, for example, about the differences between *The Last Samurai* and *Lightning Rods*, DeWitt has discussed them in terms of the rhetoric characteristic of different genres: "My sense is that 'round/flat' doesn't really capture the difference between characters in *Samurai* and in *Lightning Rods*; the difference seems to be a matter of genre, hence of different styles of rhetoric. The characters in *Samurai* invite an emotional investment that the characters in *Lightning Rods* do not, which is simply to say that the latter is a comedy."[24]

DeWitt's rhetorical approach to composition does not dispense with expressivity but rather subordinates expressivity to the demands of genre. It also, notably, doesn't fully join the antiexpressive avant-garde. Advocating for such artistic impersonality makes sense only in a world where expressive subjectivity is a dominant ideology of art. But rhetoric long precedes the rise of this ideology and furnishes DeWitt with conceptual resources to sidestep these debates. Literature becomes a species of rhetoric for DeWitt, and the job of the ambitious artist is to play with the possibilities of genre, rhetoric, and form.

All of which is to say, the ultimate referent of Sibylla's mathematized thought—and DeWitt's—is *literary*. If Ludo is, as I argued in the last chapter, an uneasy metaphor for the novel itself, then a society that threatens to stifle the boy's flourishing also stifles "all [the] possibilities" of the development of the novel and art more generally. A free novel, a free art, would have the power to explore the combinatorial possibilities of form. This is not to say that a free novel would be free of constraints. Quite the opposite, in fact. As a condition of its freedom, it would work through constraints the author had chosen for herself, not those imposed by style manuals. In the battle between DeWitt and her copyeditor, freedom collides with propriety. Are the novel's limits imposed by the novelist or by those who claim the right to dictate and enforce social norms? Whose constraints predominate?

IV

In this chapter and throughout this book, I've suggested that the relationship between an author and her publisher is, ultimately, a power relationship. This power relationship reflects broader relations of power in the society within which this literary relation is embedded. And the implications of this relation are not extrinsic but intrinsic to literary study—that is to say, these relations enter the text, becoming the subject matter of the text, in a variety of ways, raising important questions for critical interpretation.

DeWitt asks: "How can we possibly assess the texts we see when we don't know the contractual restraints on the author? when we don't know whether the publisher was willing to respect the contract? when we don't know whether the author had a powerful agent or a weak one, whether the published book was substantially what the author wanted or the result of a lot of arm-twisting off-stage? Editorial comments are never made public; why not?"[25]

One might read these questions as tendentious. DeWitt's questions lean one way, suggesting that it is always or predominantly *the author* who has been compromised, that it's the editorial comments that will always or predominantly be found wanting. But reading these questions against the grain, I'd emphasize that one cannot be committed to rationality without also being committed to the possibility that one might be on the wrong side of any particular question. Perhaps this or that contractual restraint makes sense or is justified. Perhaps an author has a weak agent because they aren't producing books readers want to buy, and perhaps strong agents are strong because they have a good sense of what will and won't sell.[26] And perhaps an editorial comment makes a lot of sense. My goal here isn't to apportion blame but to endorse the larger point DeWitt makes. A sociologically minded critic cannot assess a text without knowing the institutional contexts of its production and the power relations that shape those contexts. Copyediting is one of many vectors through which such power relations shape texts, and it was a crucial vector for DeWitt, whose conception of literary art, informed by her training in classics and interest in rhetoric, was aimed at exploring literary forms that existing social relations and critical standards of propriety ignored or disavowed.

Such battles—between those who advocate for the freedom of the author and those who uphold standards of propriety or the rights of the publisher—are nothing new in the history of literature. They frequently feature in heroic stories we tell about Romantic, bohemian, modernist, and avant-garde artistic practices. Such stories often cast the artist as lone hero and the publisher as censorious villain. To be sure, DeWitt probably sees herself as the hero of her own story, and she has little to say in praise of editors, agents, and publishers. But to my mind, such negotiations between artists and middlemen are inescapable. They're always a condition of possibility to produce art of any sort, and the question for critics is how such contexts become more than conditions of possibility— that is, how they become relevant for interpretation.

In the case of *The Last Samurai*, DeWitt's mathematized reimagining of the history of the novel serves expressive ends. If following *The Chicago Manual of Style* is a metanorm—one follows it because that is what is done—we might say that copyediting, or the culture of copyediting, was not only a fetter for DeWitt but also, perhaps unwittingly, her very subject. That is, DeWitt follows the playful example of Oulipo, but she sets her sights not on pure form but rather on the normative restrictions that constrain expression.

The fight for the future of literature happens in specific judgments about usage, orthography, and style. In this fight, we can see how DeWitt's approach to writing differs from more conventional approaches to experimental and literary writing. The creative writing program nominally asks writers to "write what they know," a mantra whose many nuances Mark McGurl has analyzed at length in *The Program Era*, his important study of the rise of creative writing.[27] By contrast, DeWitt begins procedurally, asking what language and literature knows—and what they can do. A voice captures her, and she's off to the races. What are the possibilities of this form? How does one make this idea work? What story might we retroactively whip up to justify this or that charming formal premise? *What if. . . what if. . . what if. . .?*

Some version of this method is familiar to students of literary experimentalism and the avant-garde, and we have seen its resonances with

Oulipo and conceptual art more generally. But DeWitt doesn't fit easily into these well-studied traditions. She isn't primarily combating habituated thought, as many modernists did, or using literature to engage directly in social criticism, as many postmodernists did. Nor is she primarily concerned with the way that postmodern habits of mind have made sincerity, communication, and human connection more difficult. That is, she's not, as I thought, many years ago, quite like postpostmodernists such as David Foster Wallace and Zadie Smith.

DeWitt is, instead, a contemporary student of classical rhetoric. Her eye is not so much on the present as on the distant past and the far future. She sees historical possibilities that have been forgotten and loves to speculate on what might yet be possible. A fan of Michael Lewis's business book *Moneyball: The Art of Winning an Unfair Game*, DeWitt roots for underutilized forms, forms that sit on the bench of literary history, rendered invisible by conventional thought, corrupt priorities, or lack of imagination. The fantasy at the heart of *Moneyball* is that statistical rigor might help cut through the fog, might render hidden values newly visible. DeWitt's outlier status—her artistic singularity—partly explains her conflicts with the publishing establishment. It possibly also explains why academics have not shown much interest in her fiction. DeWitt doesn't fit into the existing periodizing boxes critics of contemporary literature tend to rely on. Considering these periodizing categories will open what will be the final horizon of our analysis of the story of the making of *The Last Samurai*—the horizon of deep time.

5

THE BEST BOOK OF THE
FORTY-FIFTH CENTURY

I

After a few last-minute delays, *The Last Samurai* was published in late November 2000. DeWitt didn't want a big launch party. Following her fight with her copyeditor, she was no longer feeling entirely sane. She was afraid she might melt down publicly, so she wanted a small celebration. Her collaborators had other ideas. A big party was in the offing. Tina Brown was convinced to host the launch of *The Last Samurai* at her apartment in Manhattan. DeWitt didn't want Tina Brown to lose face or to sabotage her own book's launch, so she flew from the United Kingdom to the United States. But when she arrived, she didn't want to talk to anyone, including her friends Tim Schmidt and Maude Chilton. She stayed in a hotel in Washington, DC, near Dupont Circle and recalls buying books—including a copy of Erving Goffman's *Asylums*—at Kramerbooks & Afterwords. She would sit in her hotel room and read all day, which she found comforting. "He's very good on damaged identity and the damaged mind," she told me, speaking of Goffman. She was, she said, in the grip of "madness." She tried to describe the nature of the madness she felt to me. It felt, she said, as if an alien were controlling her body.[1] DeWitt attended the party in New York without incident and left the city again, going to Philadelphia, missing a meeting with her new agent Andrew Wylie, and reading alone in the library until her next obligation—a screening of *Seven Samurai* in New York. Everyone was furious at her for disappearing.

In an unpublished journal entry, which she shared with me, DeWitt describes the nature of madness in slightly different terms. "People who are not insane tend not to know what it looks like. They tend not to know the real source of terror." "The real source of terror," she writes, "is the fact that no matter how bad things get you are always the one who has to deal with them."[2] In time, she would be the only one left to deal with the fallout of her experience publishing *The Last Samurai* with Talk Miramax. By the end of 2000, many of the bets the Weinstein brothers had placed were going bad. The company's "singular cultural status," the film historian Alisa Perren writes, began to be tarnished at the turn of the millennium, and its "ability to sell itself as independent or as a young upstart became less and less tenable."[3] *Talk* magazine survived until February 2002. In 2005, the Weinsteins would leave Miramax to start the Weinstein Company, and they founded a new book imprint, Weinstein Books. When they left, they still owned a stake in Talk Miramax Books, and they made an agreement with Disney to retain a financial interest in books published through September 30, 2007.[4] Jonathan Burnham left in 2005 to become the head of the Harper imprint at HarperCollins.[5] Talk Miramax was ultimately folded into Hyperion, and in time Hyperion was acquired by French publisher Hachette (itself a subsidiary of the multinational media conglomerate Lagardère Group), which renamed Hyperion "Hachette Books." In 2009, Weinstein Books entered a joint venture with Perseus Books, and in 2016 the imprint was also acquired by Hachette. In 2017, after accusations of sexual assault were brought against Harvey Weinstein, Weinstein Books was dissolved.

The experiment of Talk Miramax ultimately failed. The books it published scattered to the wind and today are largely forgotten. Though it was well received by many critics at the time of publication, *The Last Samurai* went out of print. The book was published in twenty languages, but DeWitt struggled to get paid what she thought she was due from foreign publishers. She hired the Wylie Agency, hoping they would skillfully manage foreign rights for her, but she ultimately had a high-profile falling out with the agency. DeWitt wrote a strongly critical comment in the comments section of an interview with Andrew Wylie in 2007. "AW's account of his agency bears no resemblance to my experience of the service offered," she wrote. "The chaos engendered by this style of organization drove me to a complete breakdown."[6] U.S. rights to *The Last Samurai* reverted to DeWitt, and after the critical success of *Lighting Rods*, New Directions republished a second edition of *The Last Samurai* in 2016 to acclaim.

The arc of literary history bends toward oblivion. Most authors do not find readers. Among those that do, most struggle to make ends meet. And even authors who find sustainable forms of literary success cannot hold a candle to the success of artists in other arenas of the culture industry. There's a reason many contemporary authors today aspire to join the writer's room, perhaps as a show runner.[7] As Amy Hungerford argues, "Literary and cultural ideas can be wiped into the invisible region of the recent past when any literary enterprise fails to gain customers, when commercial rent goes up, when a conglomerate cuts costs, when a grant is not bestowed, when a job is lost, when love or friendship or illness or birth or prejudice disrupts the social circumstances upon which a project depends."[8] These moments of failure seem, almost tautologically, to exist outside literary history, but they are in fact the very substance that literary history is made of. Many writers strive to create something of lasting value. Overwhelmingly, they fail. They fail, and they fail, and they fail again. And even if they succeed, as William Deresiewicz observes, they increasingly fail to get paid.[9] Cute invocations of Beckett aside, most artists don't get to fail better a second time, let alone a third. They just fail, full stop. Publishers, too, come and go. In the slurry of mergers and acquisitions, the original connotation of a storied literary imprint usually gets pulverized. Other than a handful of authors, literary critics, psychoanalysts, and publishing professionals—who feels anything for Hogarth Press today? Most publishing stories end like the story of Talk Miramax. Literary scholarship that doesn't account for this churn fails to contextualize those whom critics deem successful or to understand the role contingency plays in the success of works we take to have enduring value. If but for a slightly different set of initial conditions, you would not have heard of your favorite author. Other writers, who lived or live in grinding obscurity, might instead have an audience.

The odds are stacked against all authors. Almost none succeed, and even successful writers live near the borderlands of oblivion. So what are the chances that *The Last Samurai*, for all that it has to offer, might survive? Vanishingly small. Yet despite the many challenges DeWitt endured, *The Last Samurai* survives. From the perspective of other writers who seek and fail to find readers, it might be regarded as a smashing success. It did sell a hundred thousand copies and was translated into twenty languages. It's widely understood to be a great book—correctly in my view. And unlike almost every other book ever published, it remains in print.

Though the novel has, by many metrics, been successful, it has not necessarily been successful in the terms or on the scale DeWitt herself imagined. In the afterword to the New Directions edition of the novel, DeWitt suggested:

It's not hard to imagine a world where the effect of the book on what has been a coterie of readers is multiplied to the point where general assumptions about what is possible are changed. We have only to imagine a world where Oprah Winfrey picks up *The Last Samurai*. Or a world where a bookseller presses *The Last Samurai* upon President Obama. A world where Terry Pratchett is my very dear friend and sees *The Last Samurai* as a stand-in for Miss Susan. (I could again go endlessly on.)

(484)

DeWitt articulates a wild, maximalist hope for her book, which speaks to the scale of her ambition as a writer. Most authors prefer to sell more rather than fewer copies of the books they write. They want more rather than fewer readers, to sell books and even to make money, which might help them write more books. But I'd highlight the scale and the specificity of the effect DeWitt wants to have on her readers. She wants an Oprah-sized audience, but not merely to earn more money. What is wild about her hope isn't that she wants to find a big audience but that she wants to change the "general assumptions" of her audience. To improve them. If in Sibylla's view *Seven Samurai* teaches viewers the value of rational thought, *The Last Samurai* similarly aspires to offer readers a window onto the ease with which they too, like Ludo, can learn Greek and Japanese.

Describing her ambition for her self-published collaborative novel *Your Name Here*, DeWitt compared the book to *The Lord of the Rings*:

> Tolkien wrote *The Lord of the Rings* to provide a setting of loss, war and exile for languages he invented as a hobby; by 2003 100 million copies of the books had been sold!!!! If an alter-Tolkien had done for the languages of the Middle East what Tolkien did for the languages of the elves and the dwarves, we couldn't have the unholy mess we have now!!!!!!
>
> GRIDNEFF: So the point is to get the *message* across, without saying in so many *words*: You stupid fucking *morons*, you're learning fucking *elf* languages!
>
> DEWITT: Exactly. Exactly. it's about building bridges. It's about getting people to see that Arabic is something everyone can enjoy, it's not just for specialists, it's something that can appeal to a character they can identify with [i.e. a manipulative, calculating, promiscuous drink and drug fiend, an engaging potential serial killer].[10]

This is a comedic exchange, yes, but also dead serious. DeWitt aspires to find a readership on the scale of hundreds of millions in part because she subscribes to an instrumental and didactic vision for what art is capable of. We apparently think, for example, learning Arabic is difficult not because it's actually that difficult. No, we're afraid of learning Arabic because we're trapped within a normative horizon that leads us to underrate our capabilities!

We might have reason to doubt the truth of this claim. We might argue, for example, that the idea that a novel might lead a mass of people to learn ancient Greek or Japanese or Arabic is an implausible fantasy. If an alter-Tolkien did for the "languages of the Middle East" what our actual Tolkien did for the languages of the elves and dwarves, only a small coterie of superfans would know the languages of the Middle

East today, which would, one must admit, be a slight improvement on our actual contemporary situation.

DeWitt seems to understand the implausibility of her fantasy. After all, her body of writing is nothing if not a litany of all the normative and institutional barriers that make it unlikely, if not impossible, for *The Last Samurai* to change the general assumptions of its audience. If Oprah or Obama were to embrace the novel, we'd have reason to suspect that DeWitt's nightmarish struggle with middlemen would grow only more nightmarish. Indeed, DeWitt's fiction presupposes and is structured around the allure and implausibility of this fantasy of reception. The willing mass audience for DeWitt's language instruction doesn't currently exist, and if it came to exist—and if we found ourselves living in a world where a hundred million people were ready to receive such a message— the didactic elements of DeWitt's novel would, in many ways, be moot. Those hundred million would already be tearing through kanji flash cards and highlighting Arabic newspapers in their spare time. What *The Last Samurai* showcases, in a variety of ways, are the circumstances that make its own ideal reception difficult, if not impossible. DeWitt's proposal— that we're capable of more than we recognize   exposes the institutional forces that interfere with our ability to develop our capabilities. Yet this way of writing creates a significant cleavage between her actual audience and her imagined audience. In the pages of this final chapter, I want to ask who DeWitt's imagined audience is and what creating a portrait of this audience can tell us about the ambition of *The Last Samurai*—and its place in literary history.

II

Early in the novel, DeWitt constructs a metaphor that indirectly pictures the book's relationship to its readers. During a conversation with Liberace, Sibylla suggests that an urgent task for writers at the end of the twentieth century is to create new Rosetta Stones. The original Rosetta Stone was, let us recall, an inscribed stone found by the Nile in the eighteenth century, which contained the same text written in three scripts—the hieroglyphic and demotic scripts of ancient Egyptian and ancient Greek. Its discovery enabled scholars to decipher hieroglyphics. On the evening of the one-night stand that results in Ludo's conception, walking through the Mayfair district of London, Sibylla explains to Liberace that "we need more" Rosetta Stones (65).

When Liberace asks what this might mean, Sibylla explains that "probably one day English will be a much-studied dead language; we should use this fact to preserve other languages to posterity. You could have Homer with translation and marginal notes on vocabulary and grammar so that if that single book happened to be dug up in 2,000 years or so the people of the day would be able to read Homer, or better yet, we could disseminate the text as widely as possible to give it the best possible chance of survival" (65).

Sibylla also proposes that legislation might be formulated "to have, say, a page of Sophocles or Homer in the original with appropriate marginalia bound into the binding, so that even if you bought an airport novel if your plane crashed you would have something to reread on the desert island" (65). This fanciful legislation might, Sibylla speculates, also benefit present-day readers, helping to disseminate knowledge of Greek. "The great thing," she explains, "is that people who were put off Greek at school would then have another chance," and they would learn that Greek is "not a particularly difficult language" (65). One would be hard pressed to find a constituency interested in passing legislation to preserve dead languages in this way, but Sibylla's fantasy highlights the disjunction between the time horizon of electoral institutions and lawmaking bodies and the time horizon of empires and civilizations. Our institutions, in short, are revealed to be poorly calibrated to think about such ambitious scales or to undertake such self-conscious projects of preservation. Liberace's evident lack of imagination, his bland response to Sibylla's inventive proposals, is of course meant to be a sign that he would be an inadequate father for a child as gifted as Ludo.

These new Rosetta Stones would, in one stroke, preserve ancient languages and classic works of literature for future generations. The contemporary novel, reimagined as a Rosetta Stone, reconfigures cultural capital, grafting what is thought to have timeless value (the works of Sophocles or Homer) onto the trivial or the trashy (the airport novel). It's a vehicle for preserving important works of art and ancient languages but is also a tactic for confronting present-day connoisseurs of the trivial with serious literature, which they might appreciate if they had adequate time (if they were, say, stranded on a desert island). In Sibylla's fantasy, this grafting of cultural registers—the fusing of high and low—is a matter of binding one text (the high) physically to another (the low).

The Last Samurai, we are led to understand, might be something like one of these new Rosetta Stones. In DeWitt's hands, Sibylla's fantasy gets reconfigured, and the project of making new Rosetta Stones becomes the project of inventing a new literary form, a kind of book that mixes cultural registers within the text, that serves a didactic function, driving home for the reader the ease with which she might, like Ludo, come to master Greek, Japanese, or Old Norse. Indeed, though the book doesn't incorporate Sophocles or Homer into its binding, it includes extensive discussions of Attic Greek, Japanese, and other languages, and the book ultimately invites us to read it with two sets of eyes. First, we read as present-day readers who might be delighted to learn the news that, at the same time we're reading an entertaining narrative, we're also picking up new languages. We're simultaneously asked to imagine the perspective of a future civilization that might happen upon the text of the novel and through the medium of the novel look back onto our time.

The project of creating new Rosetta Stones also speaks to the larger pedagogical aesthetic of *The Last Samurai*. It's a novel that wants to teach us something. But it's also a time capsule of what it is and isn't possible to teach those who live under contemporary conditions. Indeed, Sibylla ostensibly writes her novel as a record, for the distant future, of the life of a boy who might be both a genius and a prodigy. "If L comes to good not by some miracle but by doing the right thing rather than the wrong," Sibylla reasons, "others may profit from his escape; if he comes to bad (as is not unlikely) his example may spare them" (29). Like DeWitt, Sibylla is putting herself into a relation not only with her contemporaries but also larger horizons of time.

As DeWitt elsewhere observes, "The writer's intellectual formation . . . draws on textual relations with humans who may have lived any time in the last several millennia."[11] But the body of the writer, inevitably, is contemporary with other bodies, and those bodies are embedded in specific social institutions.

We really have no chance of being contemporaries of our own contemporaries, even if we want to—if we stick with the conventional publishing model. Books I wrote or started last year, five years ago, 10 years ago, might get into the public domain in 2012, 2022, or never. The determining factor is not the quality of the books; it's the extent to which Helen DeWitt can marshal the social skills, the obstinacy, the willingness to suspend writing indefinitely to wheel and deal, to get the fuckers into print.

It's contemporary institutions—and the norms, logic, and priorities they enforce—that make it difficult or impossible to stand in a relation with one's contemporaries. Having a textual relationship to the past or the far future, it turns out, seems far more tractable.

III

The Last Samurai has a conflicted relationship to its own time, a conflicted relationship to different hypothetical audiences. The novel seems both to intervene in its own moment—to break through an obstacle course of institutional barriers, desperate to reach contemporary audiences— and to give up on its own time, to prefer a relationship to the distant past and the distant future. The novel's temporal shearing is unique—but speaks to larger questions about how we study contemporary literature and how we *should* study it. Throughout this book, I've given a lot of attention to the immediate contexts that shaped DeWitt's novel, arguing that they not only hobbled *The Last Samurai* but also, in different ways, enabled it—becoming the very subject matter of the book. Yet some might dispute my methodological priority. They might argue that the scale of my analysis should either be enlarged or shrunk. Surely, the value of *The Last Samurai* transcends the contingencies of the frivolous now. Surely, the novel should be contextualized in a way that looks beyond the limitations of the publishing industry in the late 1990s. Noting Sibylla's attachment to the idea of creating new Rosetta Stones, one might argue that *The Last Samurai* itself seems to offer support for such a critique. That is, the sociological mode of analysis I've adopted might seem vulnerable to recent criticisms of historicism (which is arguably a superset of the method I adopt).

Historicism is a method that has a long history and has long been an object of debate by literary critics. I use the term to refer to the thesis, as Ted Underwood describes it, that "different ages were separated by profoundly different, perhaps mutually incomprehensible, modes of life and thought."[12] This is a highly stylized description of historicism, one that papers over many detailed debates, but it serves my purposes well enough. In literary criticism, the historicist thesis comes with a corollary claim that literature uniquely captures the lost spirit of prior ages, confronting the present reader with fundamentally different historical milieus. Considered in the light of this corollary, historicism becomes both an interpretive method, where the critic's job is to help us grasp the fundamental difference of the past, and a standard of aesthetic value, where the value of a literary work is partly connected to the way it captures the spirit of its age. Fredric Jameson once proposed the slogan "Always historicize!" as the ultimate imperative of literary criticism, and he argued that "only Marxism can give us an adequate account of the essential *mystery* of the cultural past, which, like Tiresias drinking the blood, is momentarily returned to life and warmth and allowed once more to speak, and to deliver its long-forgotten message in surroundings utterly alien to it."[13] Jameson's relationship to historicism is complex—and the verb *to historicize* is not for him a synonym with the noun *historicism*—but here he assumes that the cultural past is fundamentally different, "utterly alien," from our moment.

Jameson sought to defend the validity of his focus on history from poststructuralist critiques, which argued that historical moments don't possess a unity or coherence.[14] Jameson largely succeeded in his defense, even as some prominent literary critics have more recently argued that historicism forecloses other interpretive methods and aesthetic standards. Nonetheless, historicist assumptions remain prevalent both in the academy and the wider culture. At the least, the *New York* magazine critics who anointed *The Last Samurai* as the best book of the century seem to hold fast to a popular version of the historicist thesis. In his opening essay, *New York*'s books editor Boris Kachka suggests that the project of creating a twenty-first-century canon may appear "arbitrary," yet the "time frame [of the list] is not quite as random as it may seem."[15] In fact, the "aughts and teens represent a fairly coherent cultural period, stretching from the eerie decadence of pre-9/11 America to the presidency of Donald Trump."[16] This "mini-era packed in the political, social, and cultural shifts of the average century," including "wars, economic collapse, permanent-seeming victories for the once excluded, and the vicious backlash under which we currently shudder." Illuminated by this recent historical light, the books on the list turn out to be, for all their variety, "about instability," which is the "hallmark of the era after the 'end of history' that we call now."

An age of instability, it seems, calls for a literature of instability. Kachka doesn't speak for every critic who participated in this canon-making exercise, nor is every book listed easily assimilated to the category of "instability." (Is "instability" a political category? A psychological category? An aesthetic category?) But the effort to make fidelity to headline events a standard of literary value is a loosely theorized pop version of historicism, one that academic critics also engage in more often than we might prefer to admit. This pop historicism assumes that the job of the writer is to codify the spirit of the age *for* the age. For every development of the new century—Y2K, the dot-com crash, the terrorist attacks of September 11, 2001, the War on Terror, the subprime financial crisis, the Obama presidency, the election of Donald Trump, the coronavirus pandemic, Russia's invasion of Ukraine—one now expects to find a corresponding novel, each headline event casting an artistic shadow, on a two- or three-year delay.

As Alexander Manshel has shown, contemporary authors have indeed increasingly written what he calls the "recent historical novel."[17] By "recent historical novel," Manshel means novels that set their stories in the "very recent past," as opposed to an unspecified continuous present. We can read many 9/11 novels, or a novel set around the time of the 2004 Madrid train bombing, or a novel set during Barack Obama's 2008 campaign for president—and so on, books that might as well come with time and date stamps impressed on every page.[18] Not only does our literary culture elevate historicist novels, but inhabitants of the twenty-first century are carving history into thinner and thinner slices. On the basis of this trend, we might someday soon expect, say, every Twitter controversy to spawn a corresponding novel, codifying last week's or yesterday's lost mode of life and thought.

The Last Samurai is a book that arguably does not play well with these critical assumptions. This lack of fit with its time is, Christian Lorentzen suggests, part of what made critics and readers slow to recognize DeWitt's achievement. A book that seeks to explain our time to the far future may take our time as its subject, but surely it has bigger ambitions than merely representing this or that mode of life. Yet it would be misleading to claim that The Last Samurai straightforwardly fulfills its own posthistoricist ambition. For all its conceptual pyrotechnics, the novel is not a Rosetta Stone but very much a book of our time, one whose struggle to escape its time, to resist the temptations of an easy pop historicism or straightforward topicality, might be taken to be perfectly characteristic of our moment.

Some critics have recently questioned the premises of historicism with renewed vigor. Caroline Levine and Joseph North, to name two, have criticized what they call the "historicist/contextualist paradigm."[19] Levine criticizes historicism by suggesting that critics should not focus only on what literary texts mean but study what they can do in the world. North, meanwhile, rejects the current practice of literary criticism, which claims to produce new kinds of knowledge about the world. He calls instead for a criticism committed to "cultivating new ranges of sensibility, new modes of subjectivity, new capacities for experience."[20] Wai Chee Dimock, meanwhile, has suggested that the problem with historicism is the scale or resolution at which it imagines history operating, and she argues that we should put American literature into a temporally longer and more globally distributed frame. "Literature is the home of nonstandard space and time," she writes.[21]

Doesn't DeWitt's novel perfectly align with the priorities of these critics? Doesn't *The Last Samurai* conceive of the novel as a technology that might change the sensibility of the reader, that might make connections and implant itself not in the fleeting instant, but in deep time? Or, as DeWitt herself puts it, "The writer's intellectual formation . . . draws on textual relations with humans who may have lived any time in the last several millennia." DeWitt's book did, after all, come out on top of the *New York* canon, no doubt in part because of the support of writers and editors associated with *n+1*, a prestigious little magazine whose editors have criticized the dominance of historicist sociology in the style of Pierre Bourdieu.[22]

As a somewhat bemused historicist might note, attacks on historicism are themselves very much "in the air," part of our intellectual mode of life, both in and out of the academy, at the turn of the millennium. All of which is to say that *The Last Samurai* is more a book of its time than it or than critics of an antihistoricist bent might want to admit. As Edwin Turner writes on the book blog *Biblioklept*:

> While I don't endorse Wood's scolding use of the phrase "hysterical realism," I do think that it's a useful (if perhaps too-nebulous) description for a set of trends in some of the major novels published in the late nineties and early 2000s: *Infinite Jest, Middlesex, The Corrections, A Heartbreaking Work of Something or Other*, etc. And, to come in where I started: *The Last Samurai* shares a lot of the same features with these texts—the blending of styles and texts and disciplines, etc. DeWitt's filtering a lot of the same stuff, I guess. I would maybe use the term *post-postmodernism* in place of "hysterical realism" though—although a novel need not be subsumed by any term, and maybe the best can't really be described in language at all.[23]

Turner's periodization doesn't seem wrong to me, though the method of periodization, where each era is defined by what it "filters," might be developed more fully. We might endlessly debate whether a novel participates in or deviates from a specific cultural trend, and Turner allows himself the escape hatch that "the best" don't fit easily into these trends. What I would have us focus on is the way *The Last Samurai* incorporates these questions into itself. *The Last Samurai* is, in fact, largely written in English. It's built around a time-tested quest structure and has a relatively uplifting happy ending, in which Ludo's quest for a father, though it brings him into contact with danger and suffering, ultimately saves his mother—or seems likely to.

Rather than say the novel fails to live up to Sibylla's aesthetic vision, though, I'd argue DeWitt asks us to question where the boundary is between Sibylla's aesthetic ideal and DeWitt's novelistic practice. Sibylla's primary model of great art is, after all, *Seven Samurai*, and in the debate between Ludo and Sibylla mentioned in chapter 3, Ludo turns his mother's argument about art against her favorite film. Trying to find flaws in her logic, the boy suggests that by his mother's own standards *Seven Samurai* cannot be any good because "it's in black and white and Japanese" (230). Sibylla doesn't find this objection convincing, explaining, "There is an obvious difference between someone who works within the technical limitations of his time which are beyond his control and someone who accepts without thinking limitations which are entirely within his own power to set aside."

I've already discussed this dispute, but new dimensions of its meaning are visible when cast against a background of Deep Time. The distinction Sibylla makes is, I think, far from obvious. What force prevented Kurosawa from incorporating languages other than Japanese into his films? Whatever it was, it surely cannot be straightforwardly equated with the limitations that kept him from making color films (until *Dodesukaden* in 1970). And even the case of filming in color merges economic, historical, and technical questions of considerable complexity. The struggle to define the difference between technical limits within one's control and those not in one's control—the difference between being of one's time and transcending one's time—affects everyone who aspires to make art, and it's the struggle that has perhaps most defined DeWitt's career as she has navigated a literary and economic world that, as much for her as Sibylla, she feels has thwarted her flourishing. DeWitt has reacted to this literary world not by extolling her own idiosyncratic genius but by invoking a rhetoric of "rationality," which is necessarily intersubjective, asking not that institutions get out of the way but that they operate according to higher standards. The effort to move beyond one's time and place, as it turns out, requires the most ruthless scrutiny of that time and place.

If *The Last Samurai* has something to say to those of us who are not artists, it's because this same world sometimes feels as if it were designed to thwart everyone's flourishing, not just the flourishing of the artist. DeWitt's invocation of "the rational" as a figure for a better future world necessarily exceeds the boundaries of her local artistic situation. What is rational cannot, if one takes rationality as a standard seriously, be just a tendentious synonym for what is good *for her.* That is, her specific complaints—editors have misread her words, her contract isn't being honored, etc.—must also require us to inquire how we might organize a society according to standards designed to address *everyone's* specific complaints. By this standard of reckoning, the freedom of the individual artist is inseparable from the freedom of everyone else. If *The Last Samurai* is a great novel, its greatness has something to do with the fact that it is one of the novels most obsessed with exploring and dramatizing the limitations that hobble ambition. DeWitt is not content, as Ben Lerner is, to suggest that every poem or novel necessarily fails in its ambition but *by failing* thereby also expresses a utopian hope for a better future, a better world.[24] Nor does DeWitt merely lament the limits placed upon artists today, letting us know—as Chad Harbach has written—that an artist is a "person whose work is shaped by education and economy and a host of other pressures, large and small."[25]

DeWitt tries more than almost any other contemporary novelist actually to challenge the existing conventions, assumptions, and norms that circulate in our literary field. She focuses her attention—and ours—squarely on the technical, ideological, and political limitations of our time and makes us aware of the degree to which we are, in one way or another, squandering our potential. She makes the limits on her art the content of her art. But in doing so, *The Last Samurai* does not so much reinforce or prop up the antihistoricist polemics of Levine, North, or the editors of *n+1* as showcase the constraints that make escaping history difficult. She also holds hope, perhaps irrational hope, for what she might call a more rational future, a future in which there is an alignment between the idiosyncratic needs of the individual artist and the social institutions, norms, and readerly habits of mind that bring the artist's work into public consciousness.

IV

Two decades have passed since *The Last Samurai* was first published. Its persistence suggests that it might survive to find new readers in the twenty-second century. It will, perhaps, stand as a testament to the role that art plays in both showcasing the limitations of our moment and providing comfort in the face of destruction. It's a novel that looks forward to a better future, a day when the struggles it so vividly dramatizes will be historical curiosities. Did you know that—once, not too long ago—single mothers struggled to make ends meet and give their children an education to match their talents? Did you know that children were once held in absolute economic subjection by adults into whose keeping fate had consigned them? Did you know we once hobbled, thwarted, and unmade our most talented artists, scholars, and intellectuals? Faced with such curiosities, inhabitants of that better future might remark what a strange world that must have been and might note the irony that such a world nonetheless managed to produce its share of artistic marvels.

When she describes her ambition to "strike a style to amaze," Sibylla admits:

> I think I am not likely to discover the brush of Cézanne; if I am to leave no other record I would like it to be a marvel. But I must write to be understood; how can formal perfection be saved? I see in my mind a page, I think of Cicero's *De Natura Deorum*: across the top one Latin line, the rest English (or possibly German), identification of persons obscure after 2,000 years. Just so will this look if I explain every

reference for 45th-century readers, readers who may, for all I know, know
the name of a single 21st century genius (the one now five years old).

(31)

The most important question we might ask is therefore not whether *The
Last Samurai* is the best novel of the twenty-first century but whether
there's a chance—even perhaps one chance in 500 trillion trillion trillion—
that it might be recognized as the best novel of the forty-fifth.

CODA

Through a Hole in the Wall

n 2011, Helen DeWitt published a second novel with New Directions. By all accounts, it's a pretty strange book and was generally received as a radical break from *The Last Samurai*. One can see why. *Lightning Rods* is written almost entirely in the style of popular self-help manuals. It tells the story of Joe, a hapless cliché-addled salesman who makes his fortune by commodifying his sexual fantasies. He founds a firm that sells sexual services to corporate and government clients, employing women who pose as temps, surreptitiously offering sexual services to the "highest performing" men in the office.[1] A custom-built bathroom apparatus lowers the lower bodies of these women into a handicapped toilet stall in an adjacent men's room. Male top performers proceed to fuck those sex workers from behind, thereby relieving their own desire. Thus is the problem of workplace sexual harassment solved![2]

There is much to say about *Lightning Rods*—it's a novel that deserves extended analysis, just as much as *The Last Samurai*—but I'd like to suggest, briefly, that *The Last Samurai* and *Lightning Rods* are less different than they initially seem. Both arise from DeWitt's commitment to procedural aesthetics. Both began life as thought experiments and wish-fulfillment fantasies. *The Last Samurai* took Kurosawa's *Seven Samurai* as its major intertext, while *Lightning Rods* was inspired in part by Mel Brooks's *The Producers*. And DeWitt was circulating the manuscript of *Lightning Rods* around the same time as she ended up selling *The Last Samurai*. But there are other, less obvious connections between them.

In interviews, DeWitt has suggested that her follow-up book might be read as a working through of her struggle to find a publisher for *The Last Samurai*. Speaking to a somewhat befuddled interviewer at *The Believer*, DeWitt suggests that

> *Lightning Rods* was a response to the very bad experience of having *Samurai* sent out and having all these unsolicited comments from people whom I knew nothing about. . . . My experience of that was like being fucked from behind through a hole in the wall. See, sexual abuse is taken very seriously, but intellectual abuse is not seen as a problem. . . . Anything that is just an arbitrary statement rather than something that is argued for, I perceive as degrading and insulting and being fucked from behind through a hole in the wall.[3]

In an interview with *Bookforum*, DeWitt offers a notably different mapping between *Lightning Rods* and *The Last Samurai*, noting that her second novel tells the story, after all, of "a guy who starts out selling Encyclopaedia Britannica, then moves to vacuum cleaners, and finally commodifies his sexual fantasies because there just weren't enough people buying the Encyclopaedia Britannica."[4]

Any such connections, she insists, were likely "subconscious," yet what interests me is less DeWitt's subconscious than the tensions visible in her retrospective reconstruction of that psychic allegorical machinery and the way DeWitt's self-interpretation highlights the gender politics of her relationship to the publishing industry. *Lightning Rods* depicts the convergence of office work, emotional labor, and reproductive labor—themes that have been discussed at length by critics.[5] But DeWitt's self-interpretation suggests that these themes are also intimately linked to *The Last Samurai* and have material consequences for interpreting that novel.

We might wonder whether DeWitt, by this analogy, is more like Joe, whom Sianne Ngai describes as "a white male heterosexual American personification of capital," or more like his "gimmick," the female temporary workers whose job it is to get fucked from behind.[6] Is DeWitt a boss or a worker?[7] By DeWitt's telling, it's a little bit, or some strange

mix, of both. She's both being fucked from behind by arbitrary institutional authority and innovatively finding a way to flourish in a context
disinterested in her more serious, encyclopedic literary offerings (that is,
the *Britannica*). Sex also has a dual character in these readings. It's not
only a figure for a more general, more serious form of intellectual abuse
but also an instrument of Joe's success (not to mention the success of some
of the more ambitious women who work for him).

Most recent critics have wanted to imagine DeWitt to be the person
being screwed, not the person doing the screwing, but the allegorical
ambiguity of the figure of Joe raises an important question about the
nature of DeWitt's institutional critique and the relation of that critique
to a post–financial crisis world. In short, *Lightning Rods* was written
before the 2007–2008 financial crisis, and efforts to assimilate the novel
to a contemporary anticapitalist politics runs the risk of anachronisti-
cally misreading its—and DeWitt's—critique of institutions.

One reader of an earlier draft of this book observed that DeWitt's
critique of institutions can sometimes seem rather individualistic in
nature. That is, DeWitt seems to want to defend the right of the genius
to be difficult, a demand that might, today, be hard to distinguish from
the defense of toxic colleagues and academic superstars based on their
eccentric brilliance. DeWitt would hate the flattening demands of the
human resources department, whereas today's woke critics of institutions
supposedly demand that HR uses its power to weed out toxic personalities from the workplace. To put the matter more pointedly, would Harvey
Weinstein have seen in Joe *a satirical critique* of his own bad behavior or
a positive model to emulate and endorse? After all, Joe is a wild, exuberant
success! Read this way, DeWitt might be thought to endorse a kind of
'90s fantasy of escaping from mainstream institutions. Miramax Films,
likewise, wanted to imagine itself as the very emblem of cinematic inde-
pendence and integrity, what it looks like when serious artists successfully go independent (until, of course, they're bought by Disney).[8]

I think this critique of DeWitt has some merit, but it also misses the
point of the dialectical relation between individual and collective forms
of fantasy. It misses the fact that Joe doesn't *critique* the human resources
department and its priggish demands that top performers stop harassing

female workers; instead, he *becomes* the human resources department. Through an unlikely series of adventures, his private fantasies form the new institutional horizon within which everyone comes to live and work. Joe's story highlights again the importance of the figure of "rationality" for DeWitt. When one claims that one's rights as an artist are a matter of rational dispute one also invokes a whole machinery of argumentation, adjudication, and discourse, opening oneself up to the possibility that one's position might be judged negatively. DeWitt cannot both invoke rationality, cannot demand that her actions or the actions of others that she's worked with be judged in terms of their rationality, *and* guarantee in advance that her own views are, or will be judged, correct. The will to rationality is thus also a will to opening oneself—one's most fundamental commitments, one's sense of self, one's belief about reality— up to obliteration. One who refuses to accept the claim that they might be wrong betrays any real commitment to rationality.

Rationality is, at root, an intersubjective virtue. To demand that others meet one's rationality with their own is a demand for social coordination. To ask for rationality always already is to ask for a world whose institutions support that rationality. Thus do collective institutional changes (Joe's Lighting Rods firm) emerge, necessarily, from the most self-absorbed wish-fulfillment fantasies (his private sexual fantasies). That—in the case of *The Last Samurai*—choosing your own father is, strictly speaking, impossible doesn't negate the fact that pursuing such a fantasy might also become a critique of the actually existing institution of the family.

Yet the example of Joe also highlights the ultimate limits of DeWitt's approach to the critique of institutions. The problem isn't that DeWitt is too individualistic. The limits are discernable if we think of *Lightning Rods* not as an example of how DeWitt felt while dealing directly with publishers but rather a fantasy of how DeWitt hoped *The Last Samurai* might be received and find its way in the world. That is, *Lightning Rods* is a book about a wish-fulfillment fantasy that is, in fact, a second-order wish-fulfillment fantasy. In this second-order fantasy, being fucked from behind by arbitrary authority is transmuted, as if by magic, into wild market success.

Again and again, DeWitt has suggested that what she has found most frustrating about working with publishers is the way that they are, even from a strictly capitalistic point of view, leaving money on the table, refusing to give an author they claim to value what they need to flourish and write more great, profit-making novels. Some authors, such as David Foster Wallace, DeWitt notes, suggest that we should respond to the horrors of the world by becoming more empathetic. But what if a technical solution could be found? What if some new technology might be devised that simply did away with all the horror, suffering, and abuse?[9] Which is to say that the second-order wish-fulfillment fantasy of *Lightning Rods* imagines that a technical, rather than a political, solution to DeWitt's problems might be found, some hack or gimmick or trick. It's no coincidence, then, that Joe is an entrepreneur, an embodiment of capital who nonetheless refuses to play by ossified rules, norms, and institutions (except of course the metainstitution of capital accumulation).

Joe's example, it strikes me, represents a limit to DeWitt's project. Which is not to say that we should condemn *The Last Samurai* for failing, somehow, to solve the problems that come with living under capitalism or for failing to be sufficiently anticapitalist. Far from it. Rather, as I have been arguing through this project, it is only DeWitt's rigor—the seriousness of her commitment to rationality, unlike those who provincially gather under the banner of the Rationalist Community—that highlights the limits of individual action and entrepreneurial verve. It may indeed be the case that we live in a literary world that, as Lauren Oyler writes, often "eschews explorations of ideas or arguments or form in favor of joylessly sellable plots and premises inspired by a stable of influences so obvious they aren't worth mentioning."[10] But if more contemporary writers were to take seriously DeWitt's example and were committed to moving beyond the limits of such a fallen world, they would not only experiment wildly, defy existing institutions, smash the icons of contemporary aesthetic norms, habits, and standards—they'd also organize among themselves, form a community committed to the political action necessary to build the kind of world that might, at last, be ready, in the hundreds of millions, if not more, to read a book as good as *The Last Samurai*.

ACKNOWLEDGMENTS

When I first agreed to write this book, more years ago than I care to admit, I thought, "This'll be a fun and quick project, an easy-to-write, formally unified little monograph I'll knock out in six months, a year at most, before returning to longer, more structurally difficult works of scholarship." As it turned out, writing short books can be considerably harder than writing long ones. I couldn't have completed this study without a lot of help.

I want to thank Nicholas Dames, Jenny Davidson, and Philip Leventhal for inviting me to write for Rereadings and for their patience as I figured out the right form with which to tell the story of *The Last Samurai*. Good and supportive editors are today rare. They make all the difference. Thank you. Thank you also to Monique Briones, Michael Haskell, Rob Fellman, and Arc Indexing, who all helped turn my manuscript into a book. Columbia University Press is the very emblem of the "good middleman," which every author everywhere would, in a better world, have access to.

Enormous thanks are due to Jonathan Burnham, Kristin Powers, Maude Chilton, and Tim Schmidt for answering my many questions about the making of *The Last Samurai*. David Levene kindly allowed me to interview him multiple times and provided me with a copy of "Quo Virtus? The Concept of Propriety in Ancient Literary Criticism," which included the appended epilogue I discuss in chapter 2.

I was extraordinarily lucky to have a chance to speak with Helen DeWitt for seven hours on January 7, 2019, at Leisure World, in Silver

Spring, Maryland. This book would not exist in the form it does without Helen's extremely detailed answers to my questions as well as various primary source documents she provided to me, including disks with early drafts of what was then called "The Seventh Samurai" and many handwritten notes. Helen also gave me contact information for many of her foreign editors and translators. I regret that I was not able to make better use of that information, at least in this book. The story of *The Last Samurai*'s many translations—its world tour, so to speak—has yet to be told. I may or may not be able to tell that story myself, but it should be. Thanks are due to Mary DeWitt Griffin for letting me spend so much time in her home.

As I've said, this project is, among other things, an experiment in methodology. I've sought to think through, and show in these pages, how literary criticism on contemporary literature might be written differently if it were informed by oral history and sociology. I'm grateful that I've had the opportunity to speak to so many people involved with the story of *The Last Samurai*. I see now why these methods aren't more widely adopted. Documenting even the very recent cultural past is harder than I thought it would be, and my effort to do so immediately made plain to me how much we don't know about our cultural and artistic life. Any errors of fact or infelicities of interpretation are entirely my responsibility.

Audience members at two annual meetings of the Association for the Study of the Arts of the Present (ASAP) as well as one annual conference of the Modern Language Association (MLA) gave me feedback on early versions of this project. Mod/Con, UPenn English's Modernist and Contemporary Literatures Reading Group, read a long selection of this manuscript. Thanks to Eugenia Ulanova for organizing that meeting.

Though in different time zones, Scott Selisker and Adam Kelly both offered intellectual camaraderie and pointed feedback on drafts during these socially distant days. Our conversations have convinced me that David Foster Wallace was quite wrong to dismiss the possibility of sincere and intellectually nourishing exchange via videophone. This project would be poorer if not for the detailed reports of three brilliant peer reviewers. Thanks to Merve Emre, Sangeeta Ray, Gordon Hutner, Min Hyong Song, Patricia Stuelke, Ed Finn, Molly Geidel, Sheila Liming,

Mike Miley, Matthew Luter, Ellen McCallum, Gabriel Hankins, Jim English, Sarah Evans, Adrian Anagnost, Victoria Pass, Adriana Obiols, Dan Sinykin, Laura B. McGrath, and Evan Kindley. I'm grateful to the Department of English at the University of Maryland for awarding me an Arcan Semester Research Award, which was instrumental in helping me complete this project. My colleagues at Maryland have provided me with a warm and welcoming institution to call home. Again, everyone should be so lucky. Thanks especially to Amanda Bailey, Matt Kirschenbaum, Orrin Wang, Sharada Balachandran Orihuela, and Christina Walter for your friendship, advice, and support.

Julie was, as always, a reliable source of reassurance and support over these many years. My parents and Sabrina were, also as always, supportive of my intellectual labors. And Eleanor, who was born while I was working on this project, made writing a book about a story that, among other things, dramatizes the challenge of being a good parent, not to mention the challenge of teaching one's child languages other than English, especially meaningful. I look forward to a day when she reads *The Last Samurai*—and, perhaps, this study.

NOTES

PREFACE: THE LAST SAMURAI, UNREAD

1. Helen DeWitt, *The Last Samurai* (New York: New Directions, 2016), 26. All subsequent references are cited parenthetically. Page numbers correspond to the New Directions edition.

2. Christian Lorentzen, "Publishing *Can* Break Your Heart," *Vulture*, July 11, 2016, https://www.vulture.com/2016/07/helen-dewitt-last-samurai-new-edition.html.

3. Rich Beck, "The Not-Nice Novel," *Emily Books* (blog), April 20, 2012, https://emilybooks.tumblr.com/post/21445306458/the-not-nice-novel.

4. Lauren Berlant, *Cruel Optimism* (Durham, NC: Duke University Press, 2011).

5. If you haven't read the novel, stop what you're doing and go read it right now. Don't worry—this book will still be here when you finish. Even though the novel is over five hundred pages long, it's a surprisingly fast read. If you're still here and still haven't read the novel, well, okay . . . you're more than welcome to keep reading. I've tried to make this book accessible even to those who haven't yet read the novel.

6. Amy Hungerford, *Making Literature Now* (Stanford, CA: Stanford University Press, 2016). Clayton Childress, *Under the Cover: The Creation, Production, and Reception of a Novel* (Princeton, NJ: Princeton University Press, 2019). Matthew G. Kirschenbaum, *Track Changes: A Literary History of Word Processing* (Cambridge, MA: Harvard University Press, 2016). William Deresiewicz, *The Death of the Artist: How Creators Are Struggling to Survive in the Age of Billionaires and Big Tech* (New York: Holt, 2020). Paulo Lemos Horta, *Marvellous Thieves: Secret Authors of the Arabian Nights* (Cambridge, MA: Harvard University Press, 2017); Álvaro Santana-Acuña, *Ascent to Glory: How*

"One Hundred Years of Solitude" Was Written and Became a Global Classic (New York: Columbia University Press, 2020). I was also inspired by the journalistic example of Keith Gessen, *Vanity Fair's How a Book Is Born: The Making of "The Art of Fielding"* (New York: Vanity Fair, 2011), which recounts the making of Chad Harbach's novel *The Art of Fielding* (2011).

7. Hungerford, *Making Literature Now*, 17.

8. Merve Emre, "Post-Disciplinary Reading and Literary Sociology," *Modernism/modernity* Print Plus 3, cycle 4 (February 1, 2019), https://modernism modernity.org/forums/posts/post-disciplinary-reading-and-literary-sociology.

9. M. H. Miller, "Novels from the Edge: For Helen DeWitt, the Publishing World Is a High-Stakes Game," *Observer*, December 21, 2011, https://observer .com/2011/12/novels-from-the-edge-helen-dewitt-12202011/.

1. A LITTLE POTBOILER

1. Morten Høi Jensen, "Bookforum Talks to Helen DeWitt," *Bookforum*, September 22, 2011, https://www.bookforum.com/interviews/bookforum-talks -to-helen-dewitt-8389.

2. Helen DeWitt, interview by author, January 7, 2019.

3. Helen DeWitt, "Be on the One Hand Good, and Do Not on the Other Hand Be Bad," *Paperpools* (blog), April 21, 2012, http://paperpools.blogspot .com/2012/04/be-on-one-hand-good-and-do-not-on-other.html.

4. Helen DeWitt, "September 1991," 3.5" floppy disk labeled "Backup Liberace 7-6-96 + 1Liberac (Very Early)," in a file called "1LIBERAC" (created July 27, 1996), 2.

5. T. S. Eliot, *The Waste Land* (1922), ed. Michael North (New York: Norton, 2000), 3.

6. Petronius and Seneca, *Satyricon. Apocolocyntosis*, trans. Gareth Schmeling (Cambridge, MA: Harvard University Press, 2020), 85, 87.

7. Tim Schmidt, interview by author, January 14, 2019.

8. Jensen, "Bookforum Talks to Helen DeWitt."

9. Lee Konstantinou, "It's Good to Be Pragmatic: An Interview with Helen DeWitt," *Los Angeles Review of Books*, November 21, 2011, https://lareview ofbooks.org/article/its-good-to-be-pragmatic-an-interview-with-helen -dewitt/.

10. Alisa Perren, *Indie, Inc.: Miramax and the Transformation of Hollywood in the 1990s* (Austin: University of Texas Press, 2013), 225.

11. A. S. Byatt, "The Kurosawa Kid," *New Yorker*, October 30, 2000.

12. Daniel Mendelsohn, "Boy Wonder," *New York Review of Books*, September 20, 2001.

13. Jonathan Burnham, interview by author, November 30, 2018.

14. Fiachra Gibbons, "Sexes Clash on Orange Prize," *Guardian*, May 19, 2001, https://www.theguardian.com/uk/2001/may/19/books.orangeprizeforfiction 2001.

15. Jensen, "Bookforum Talks to Helen DeWitt."

16. James Wood, "Helen DeWitt Has Your Number," *New Yorker*, June 4, 2018, https://www.newyorker.com/magazine/2018/06/04/helen-dewitt-has-your -number.

17. Christian Lorentzen, "Publishing *Can* Break Your Heart," *Vulture*, July 11, 2016, https://www.vulture.com/2016/07/helen-dewitt-last-samurai-new-edi tion.html.

18. Christian Lorentzen, "Helen DeWitt's *The Last Samurai* Is the Best Book of the Century (for Now)," *Vulture*, September 17, 2018, https://www.vulture .com/2018/09/helen-dewitt-the-last samurai.html.

19. As of this writing, only a few scholars have discussed of *The Last Samurai*. For a discussion of the novel's relationship to mathematics, see Caroline Marie and Christelle Reggiani, "Portrait of the Artist as a Mathematician," *Journal of Romance Studies* 7, no. 3 (2007): 101–10. For a discussion of the way the novel invokes film, see Jonathan Foltz, *The Novel After Film: Modernism and the Decline of Autonomy* (New York: Oxford University Press, 2017). For a discussion of the way that the novel relates to the tradition of encyclopedic fiction, see Stephen J. Burn, "Encyclopedic Fictions," in *American Literature in Transition, 1990–2000*, ed. Stephen J. Burn (Cambridge: Cambridge University Press, 2017). For a discussion of the novel's representation of the family, see Yuki Namiki, "It's a Wise Child Who Knows His Own Father: The Figure of the American Family in *The Last Samurai* and *Extremely Loud and Incredibly Close*," *Textual Practice* 34, no. 12 (2020): 2131–43.

20. Franco Moretti, *Modern Epic: The World System from Goethe to Garcia Marquez*, trans. Quintin Hoare (London: Verso, 1996), 4.

21. Sam Anderson, "When Lit Blew Into Bits," *New York*, December 6, 2009, https://nymag.com/arts/all/aughts/62514/.

22. For the canonical account of encyclopedic narrative, see Edward Mendelson, "Encyclopedic Narrative: From Dante to Pynchon," *MLN* 91, no. 6 (1976): 1267–75.

23. Steven Moore, "Swords and Syntax," *Washington Post*, September 17, 2000, https://www.washingtonpost.com/archive/entertainment/books/2000/09 /17/swords-and-syntax/1fc92ed5-4552-4e9b-81cb-694f78c17ccc/.

24. Sven Birkerts, "Literature: Snapshots from the Bridge," *U.S. Society & Values* 8, no. 1 (2003), https://web-archive-2017.ait.org.tw/infousa/zhtw/DOCS /0403/ijse/birkerts.htm.

25. Burn, "Encyclopedic Fiction," 116.

26. "Gender on the Jury," *Guardian*, June 4, 2001, http://www.theguardian.com /books/2001/jun/04/orangeprizeforfiction2001.orangeprizeforfiction.

27. Nicci Gerrard, quoted in "Gender on the Jury."

28. Quoted in Jenny Davidson, "A Conversation with Novelist Helen DeWitt," *The Awl*, October 13, 2011, https://www.theawl.com/2011/10/a-conversation -with-novelist-helen-dewitt/.

29. Davidson, "A Conversation with Novelist Helen DeWitt."

30. Brian Hurley, "Knowledge Porn: On Helen DeWitt's 'The Last Samurai,'" *The Millions*, June 13, 2016, https://themillions.com/2016/06/knowledge-porn -helen-dewitts-last-samurai.html.

31. Georg Lukács, *The Theory of the Novel* (Cambridge, MA: MIT Press, 1974), 29.

2. HELEN DEWITT'S AESTHETIC EDUCATION

1. Mieke Chew, "Helen DeWitt," *BOMB*, November 12, 2014, https:// bombmagazine.org/articles/helen-dewitt/.

2. Lee Konstantinou, "It's Good to Be Pragmatic: An Interview with Helen DeWitt," *Los Angeles Review of Books*, November 21, 2011, https://lareview ofbooks.org/article/its-good-to-be-pragmatic-an-interview-with-helen -dewitt/.

3. Konstantinou, "It's Good to Be Pragmatic."

4. Francesca Schironi, *The Best of the Grammarians: Aristarchus of Samothrace on the Iliad* (Ann Arbor: University of Michigan Press, 2018), xxi.

5. On Quit Lit, see Megan Garber, "The Rise of 'Quit Lit,'" *Atlantic*, September 10, 2015, https://www.theatlantic.com/entertainment/archive/2015/09 /dont-quit-your-day-job/404671/.

6. Konstantinou, "It's Good to Be Pragmatic."

7. @helendewitt, Twitter, January 21, 2020, 12:12AM, https://twitter.com /helendewitt/status/1219487793468059649.

8. Christian Lorentzen, "Publishing *Can* Break Your Heart," *Vulture*, July 11, 2016, https://www.vulture.com/2016/07/helen-dewitt-last-samurai-new-edition.html.

9. Jenny Davidson, *Reading Style: A Life in Sentences* (New York: Columbia University Press, 2014), 15.

10. Viktor Shklovsky, *Theory of Prose*, trans. Benjamin Sher (Elmwood Park, IL: Dalkey Archive Press, 1991), 6.

11. Helen DeWitt, "Quo Virtus? The Concept of Propriety in Ancient Literary Criticism," PhD diss., Oxford University, 1987, 27.

12. DeWitt, "Quo Virtus?," 27.

13. DeWitt, "Quo Virtus?," 417a–417b.

14. DeWitt discusses Shklovsky and modernist accounts of literary innovation in her dissertation, comparing them to ancient critics. She concludes that "ancient criticism . . . has little part in the concerns of major branches of modern literary discourse." DeWitt, "Quo Virtus?," 26.

15. Nicholas Brown, *Autonomy: The Social Ontology of Art Under Capitalism* (Durham, NC: Duke University Press, 2019).

16. S. P. MacIntyre, "Helen DeWitt Interviewed by S. P. MacIntyre: Experimental, Interstitial, and Hybrid," *Mayday*, April 1, 2012, https://maydaymagazine.com/helen-dewitt-interviewed-by-s-p-macintyre-experimental-interstitial-and-hybrid/.

3. SYNERGY IS CRAP

1. "Burnham to Head Miramax/Talk Media Books," *Publishers Weekly*, November 16, 1998, https://www.publishersweekly.com/pw/print/19981116/34729-burnham-to-head-miramax-talk-media-books.html.

2. Luke O'Brien, "How to Lose $100 Million," *Politico*, May/June 2014, https://www.politico.com/magazine/story/2014/05/01/tina-brown-how-to-lose-100-million-105907/.

3. Howard Kurtz, "Tina Brown Quits the New Yorker," *Washington Post*, July 9, 1998, https://www.washingtonpost.com/archive/lifestyle/1998/07/09/tina-brown-quits-the-new-yorker/.

4. Burnham, interview by author, November 30, 2018.

5. O'Brien, "How to Lose $100 Million."

6. David D. Kirkpatrick, "At Talk Miramax, Books Offer Rare Success," *New York Times*, April 8, 2002, https://www.nytimes.com/2002/04/08/business/media-at-talk-miramax-books-offer-rare-success.html.

7. Paul Colford, "Book Bonanza for Talk Miramax," *Daily News*, February 2, 2001, http://www.nydailynews.com/archives/money/books-bonanza-talk -miramax-article-1.905995.

8. Mark L. Sirower, *The Synergy Trap: How Companies Lose the Acquisition Game* (New York: Simon and Schuster, 1997).

9. Warren St. John, "So Why Did Newhouse Sell Random House to Bertels- mann Boys?," *Observer*, March 30, 1998, https://observer.com/1998/03/so-why -did-newhouse-sell-random-house-to-bertelsmann-boys/.

10. Henry Jenkins, *Convergence Culture: Where Old and New Media Collide* (New York: New York University Press, 2008), 107.

11. I am alluding here to work by scholars such as John Thornton Caldwell, *Pro- duction Culture: Industrial Reflexivity and Critical Practice in Film and Tele- vision* (Durham, NC: Duke University Press, 2008); Jerome Christensen, *America's Corporate Art: The Studio Authorship of Hollywood Motion Pictures* (Stanford, CA: Stanford University Press, 2011); J. D. Connor, *The Studios After the Studios: Neoclassical Hollywood*, 1st ed. (Stanford, CA: Stanford Uni- versity Press, 2015); Michael Szalay, "The Incorporation Artist," *Los Angeles Review of Books*, July 10, 2012, https://lareviewofbooks.org/article/the-incor poration-artist/. With the exception of Szalay, however, this scholarship has focused primarily on film and television.

12. As Yuki Namiki notes, "This change in the mother-son relationship is rep- resented as a change in the narrative from static and circular to active and linear." Yuki Namiki, "It's a Wise Child Who Knows His Own Father: The Figure of the American Family in *The Last Samurai* and *Extremely Loud and Incredibly Close*," *Textual Practice* 34, no. 12 (2020): 2136.

13. DeWitt, interview by author, January 7, 2019.

14. Daniel Mendelsohn, "Boy Wonder," *New York Review of Books*, Septem- ber 20, 2001.

15. Clayton Childress, *Under the Cover: The Creation, Production, and Reception of a Novel* (Princeton, NJ: Princeton University Press, 2019), 11.

16. This would be part of my objection to the way that Michael Clune charac- terizes the relationship between judgment and equality in Michael W. Clune, *A Defense of Judgment* (Chicago: University of Chicago Press, 2021). See Lee Konstantinou and Dan Sinykin, "Literature and Publishing, 1945–2020," *American Literary History* 33, no. 2 (2021): 231–36.

17. The phrase "entrepreneur of the self" is from Michel Foucault, *The Birth of Biopolitics: Lectures at the Collège de France, 1978–1979* (New York: Picador,

2010). See William Deresiewicz, *The Death of the Artist: How Creators Are Struggling to Survive in the Age of Billionaires and Big Tech* (New York: Holt, 2020), for an excellent set of case studies of how artists and writers find a way to make a living under such dire circumstances.

18. This is a position Dan Sinykin and I develop further in "Literature and Publishing, 1945–2020."

19. Dan N. Sinykin, "The Conglomerate Era: Publishing, Authorship, and Literary Form, 1965–2007," *Contemporary Literature* 58, no. 4 (2017): 462–91.

20. In this sense, *The Last Samurai* is an example of what I have called "postirony" and what Adam Kelly calls "New Sincerity." See Lee Konstantinou, *Cool Characters: Irony and American Fiction* (Cambridge, MA: Harvard University Press, 2016). See also Adam Kelly, "The New Sincerity," in *Postmodern/Postwar—and After: Rethinking American Literature*, ed. Jason Gladstone, Andrew Hoberek, and Daniel Worden (Iowa City: University of Iowa Press, 2016), 197–208. That said, I would also argue that there are significant differences between DeWitt and her generational peers. See chapter 5.

21. William F. Hansen, *Anthology of Ancient Greek Popular Literature* (Bloomington: Indiana University Press, 1998), 134–35.

22. Mark C. Gridley, *Jazz Styles: Pearson New International Edition*, 11th ed. (Essex: Pearson, 2014), 168.

23. @helendewitt, Twitter, August 26, 2020, https://twitter.com/helendewitt /status/1254366890828484608.

24. Though many authors did succeed at making a name for themselves through self-publication in the 1990s. See Kinohi Nishikawa, "Driven by the Market: African American Literature After Urban Fiction," *American Literary History* 33, no. 2 (2021): 320–49.

4. FUCK *THE CHICAGO MANUAL OF STYLE*

1. DeWitt, interview by author, January 7, 2019.

2. When I asked Burnham about this episode, he commented that he'd forgotten about going to the ballet with DeWitt. He's "a big one for leaving in intervals," he wrote. He said that he presumes he "just got out [of the taxi] in lower Manhattan and let her continue to Brooklyn." More broadly, he confirmed that he and DeWitt were at odds over the copyediting of the book and writes that "I now see I was wrong." Jonathan Burnham, email to author, March 29, 2022.

3. DeWitt, interview by author, January 7, 2019.

4. DeWitt, interview by author, January 7, 2019.

5. DeWitt does something similar in her short story collection *Some Trick*. She writes, "Stories set in the UK follow British usage; stories set in the USA mostly follow American. However, when America is viewed through British eyes (for example, in 'My Heart Belongs to Bertie'), British usage will be found." Helen DeWitt, *Some Trick: Thirteen Stories* (New York: New Directions, 2018).

6. DeWitt, interview by author, January 7, 2019.

7. See also @helendewitt, Twitter, March 14, 2021, 1:22PM, https://twitter.com /helendewitt/status/1371120203199811588. Burnham confirmed that Joe Dolce helped persuade him to change his stance on the copyediting process. Burnham, email to author, March 29, 2022.

8. M. H. Miller, "Novels from the Edge: For Helen DeWitt, the Publishing World Is a High-Stakes Game," *Observer*, December 21, 2011, https://observer .com/2011/12/novels-from-the-edge-helen-dewitt-12202011/.

9. Almost undiscussed, but not entirely undiscussed, though most scholarly discussions are more focused on what we might call *developmental editing* rather than *copyediting*. See Abram Foley, *The Editor Function: Literary Publishing in Postwar America* (Minneapolis: University of Minnesota Press, 2021); as well as Tim Groenland, *The Art of Editing: Raymond Carver and David Foster Wallace* (New York: Bloomsbury, 2019).

10. Jonathan Glover, *Causing Death and Saving Lives: The Moral Problems of Abortion, Infanticide, Suicide, Euthanasia, Capital Punishment, War, and Other Life-or-Death Choices* (London: Penguin UK, 1990), 176.

11. Glover, *Causing Death and Saving Lives*, 174.

12. Caroline Marie and Christelle Reggiani, "Portrait of the Artist as a Mathematician," *Journal of Romance Studies* 7, no. 3 (2007): 109.

13. Anna Kornbluh, *The Order of Forms: Realism, Formalism, and Social Space*, 1st ed. (Chicago: University of Chicago Press, 2019), 7.

14. There are many posts on DeWitt's blog, *paperpools*, that mention R. The earliest I have found is Helen DeWitt, "losing the plot," *paperpools* (blog), May 18, 2008, http://paperpools.blogspot.com/2008/05/losing-plot.html.

15. DeWitt, *Some Trick*, 27.

16. Helen DeWitt, "Sexual Codes of the Europeans in Evergreen Review," *paperpools* (blog), August 25, 2017, http://paperpools.blogspot.com/2017/08 /sexual-codes-of-europeans-in-evergreen.html.

17. Helen DeWitt, "Sexual Codes of the Europeans: A Preliminary Report," *Evergreen Review*, Winter 2017, https://evergreenreview.com/read/sexual -codes-of-the-europeans/.

18. Weston Cutter, "An Interview with Helen Dewitt," *The Believer*, October 1, 2012, https://believermag.com/an-interview-with-helen-dewitt/.

19. Gérard Genette, *Palimpsests: Literature in the Second Degree*, trans. Channa Newman and Claude Doubinsky (Lincoln: University of Nebraska Press, 1997), 40.

20. Andrew Goldstone, *Fictions of Autonomy: Modernism from Wilde to de Man* (Oxford: Oxford University Press, 2013), 107.

21. Joshua Clover, "The Technical Composition of Conceptualism," in *Literature and the Global Contemporary*, ed. Sarah Brouillette, Mathias Nilges, and Emilio Sauri (London: Palgrave Macmillan, 2017), 105–6.

22. See Warren F. Motte, *Oulipo: A Primer of Potential Literature* (Funks Grove, IL: Dalkey Archive Press, 1998), 27.

23. I discuss DeWitt's views of genius in Lee Konstantinou, "Helen DeWitt, Hand to Mouth," *Public Books*, June 22, 2018, http://www.publicbooks.org /helen-dewitt-hand-to-mouth/.

24. Cutter, "An Interview with Helen Dewitt."

25. "An Interview with Helen DeWitt," *If: Book*, December 27, 2008, http:// futureofthebook.org/blog/2008/12/27/an_interview_with_helen_dewitt/.

26. See Laura McGrath, "Literary Agency," *American Literary History* 33, no. 2 (2021): 350–70.

27. Mark McGurl, *The Program Era: Postwar Fiction and the Rise of Creative Writing* (Cambridge, MA: Harvard University Press, 2009).

5. THE BEST BOOK OF THE FORTY-FIFTH CENTURY

1. DeWitt, interview by author, January 7, 2019.

2. Helen DeWitt, undated journal entry.

3. Alisa Perren, *Indie, Inc.: Miramax and the Transformation of Hollywood in the 1990s* (Austin: University of Texas Press, 2013), 209.

4. Edward Wyatt, "Disney and Weinsteins to Operate Miramax Books," *New York Times*, April 6, 2005, https://www.nytimes.com/2005/04/06/books /business/company-news-disney-and-weinsteins-to-operate-miramax-books .html.

5. Keith J. Kelly, "Miramax Books Big Moves On," *New York Post*, March 8, 2005, https://nypost.com/2005/03/08/miramax-books-big-moves-on/.

6. See Leon Neyfakh, "Helen DeWitt Trashes Andrew Wylie on Portfolio .com," *Observer*, December 27, 2007, https://observer.com/2007/12/helen -dewitt-trashes-andrew-wylie-on-portfoliocom/.

7. On the contemporary novelist's relation to the figure of the "show runner," see Michael Szalay, "The Incorporation Artist," *Los Angeles Review of Books*, July 10, 2021, https://lareviewofbooks.org/article/the-incorporation-artist/. As William Deresiewicz, *The Death of the Artist: How Creators Are Struggling to Survive in the Age of Billionaires and Big Tech* (New York: Holt, 2020), points out, streaming television is one of the more vibrant arenas of artistic production in the twenty-first century.

8. Amy Hungerford, *Making Literature Now* (Stanford, CA: Stanford University Press, 2016), 17.

9. Deresiewicz, *The Death of the Artist*.

10. Helen DeWitt and Ilya Gridneff, "Your Name Here," http://helendewitt .com/dewitt/yournameheresynopsis.html. This dialogue appears in slightly different form in Helen DeWitt and Ilya Gridneff, *Your Name Here* (self published, 2008), 9.

11. "An Interview with Helen DeWitt," *If: Book*, December 27, 2008, http:// futureofthebook.org/blog/2008/12/27/an_interview_with_helen_dewitt/.

12. Ted Underwood, *Why Literary Periods Mattered: Historical Contrast and the Prestige of English Studies* (Stanford, CA: Stanford University Press, 2013), 4.

13. Fredric Jameson, *The Political Unconscious* (Ithaca, NY: Cornell University Press, 1982), 9, 19.

14. Fredric Jameson, "Marxism and Historicism," *New Literary History* 11, no. 1 (1979): 41–73.

15. Boris Kachka, "A Premature Attempt at the 21st Century Literary Canon," *Vulture*, September 17, 2018, https://www.vulture.com/article/best-books-21st -century-so-far.html.

16. Kachka, "A Premature Attempt at the 21st Century Literary Canon."

17. Alexander Manshel, "The Rise of the Recent Historical Novel," *Post45*, September 29, 2017, https://post45.org/2017/09/the-rise-of-the-recent-historical -novel/.

18. One might also argue that historicist assumptions underlie the prestige of the *historical novel* as such. As James English has shown, novels with historical settings have become more prestigious, winning literary prizes at

greater rates than in the past. A historically remote temporal setting is increasingly the very mark of the literary. James F. English, "Now, Not Now: Counting Time in Contemporary Fiction Studies," *Modern Language Quarterly* 77, no. 3 (2016): 395–418.

19. Caroline Levine, *Forms: Whole, Rhythm, Hierarchy, Network* (Princeton, NJ: Princeton University Press, 2015); Joseph North, *Literary Criticism: A Concise Political History* (Cambridge, MA: Harvard University Press, 2017).

20. North, *Literary Criticism*, 6.

21. Wai Chee Dimock, *Through Other Continents: American Literature Across Deep Time* (Princeton, NJ: Princeton University Press, 2009), 4.

22. "Too Much Sociology," *n+1*, March 25, 2013, https://nplusonemag.com/issue -16/the-intellectual-situation/too-much-sociology/.

23. Edwin Turner, "Riff on Some Recent Reading," *Biblioklept*, December 5, 2018, https://biblioklept.org/tag/the-last-samurai/.

24. I am paraphrasing the argument Ben Lerner makes in *The Hatred of Poetry* (New York: FSG Originals, 2016).

25. Chad Harbach, "Introduction," in *MFA vs NYC: Two Cultures of American Fiction* (New York: Farrar, Strauss and Giroux, 2014), 4.

CODA. THROUGH A HOLE IN THE WALL

1. Helen DeWitt, *Lightning Rods* (New York: New Directions, 2011), 67.

2. I discuss *Lightning Rods* at greater length in "Hurricane Helen," *Los Angeles Review of Books*, November 21, 2011, https://lareviewofbooks.org/article /hurricane-helen/.

3. Weston Cutter, "An Interview with Helen Dewitt," *The Believer*, October 1, 2012, https://believermag.com/an-interview-with-helen-dewitt/.

4. Morten Høi Jensen, "Bookforum Talks to Helen DeWitt," *Bookforum*, September 22, 2011, https://www.bookforum.com/interviews/bookforum-talks -to-helen-dewitt-8389.

5. Sianne Ngai, *Theory of the Gimmick* (Cambridge, MA: Harvard University Press, 2021), 75–82.

6. Ngai, *Theory of the Gimmick*, 75.

7. For an analysis of DeWitt's relation to the history of temporary work and precarious labor more generally, see John Macintosh, "The Favor of Another: Labor and Precarity in Contemporary Fiction," PhD diss., University of Maryland, 2019.

8. Of course, Miramax's image of itself contrasted sharply with the reality, as Alisa Perren, *Indie, Inc.: Miramax and the Transformation of Hollywood in the 1990s* (Austin: University of Texas Press, 2013), shows.

9. Cutter, "An Interview with Helen DeWitt."

10. Lauren Oyler, "The Screwer and the Screwed," *The Baffler* 39 (2018), https://thebaffler.com/salvos/screwer-and-screwed-oyler.

INDEX